*Luther's*

# LARGE
# CATECHISM

*A Contemporary Translation
with Study Questions*

F. Samuel Janzow

SAINT LOUIS

Library of Congress Cataloging-in-Publication Data

Luther, Martin, 1483–1546.
    [Catechismus, Grosser, English]
    Luther's Large catechism: a contemporary translation
with study questions / F. Samuel Janzow.
        p.     cm.
    Translation of: Catechismus, Grosser.
    ISBN 0-570-03539-2
    1. Lutheran Church—Catechisms—English. I. Janzow,
F. Samuel. 1913–   . II. Title.
BX8070.L62A4 1988
238'.41—dc19                      87-37532

10     97

# Contents

# LUTHER'S LARGE CATECHISM

## Martin Luther's Preface [1530]

Our desire and our plea that others would use the Catechism as constantly as we do stem from more than trivial causes. To our regret we notice that many preachers and pastors are very neglectful of the Catechism, despising both their office and the Catechism teaching itself. In some cases the reason for this is their involvement on lofty heights of learning, but in others it is pure laziness and self-indulgence. They behave as if they are pastors or preachers for the sake of their bellies, with nothing to do but to live out their years high on the hog just as they used to do under the papacy.

They now have everything they should be teaching and preaching offered to them in easy, crystal-clear form within numerous worthwhile books—books that really are what the old manuals claimed to be, "Sermons That Preach Themselves," "Sleep Soundly, Your Worries Are Over," "All Is Prepared," and "Treasury of Teaching and Preaching Aids." Yet they do not have enough principle and integrity to buy the books, or having acquired them, to look them over and read them. Such disgraceful gluttons and belly servers would make better swineherds and dog trainers than watchers over souls and shepherds of Christ's flock.

They are liberated from the useless, burdensome, mechanical rote of the seven canonical hours. If in place of them, morning, noon, and evening, they would only read at least a page or two from the Catechism, prayer book, New Testament, or other section of the Bible, and pray the Lord's Prayer for themselves and their people, then they would show that they honor and are thankful for the Gospel, through which they were relieved from so many burdens and troubles. They might then also feel a little ashamed that they remembered no more of the Gospel than this their lazy, destructive, shameful, fleshly liberty of the sort that pigs and dogs enjoy. It is unfortunate that people take the Gospel altogether too lightly as it is, and that despite our best efforts we accomplish but little. What then will the result be if they see us continue being as negligent and lazy as we used to be under the papacy?

In addition, we have become infected by a vicious and insidious plague. There are many who are so satisfied with themselves and so bored with God's truths that they regard the Catechism as such a simple and slight instrument of instruction that they can rapidly read it through once and immediately have it all absorbed and mastered. Having read it through once, they throw it into a corner, as if ashamed to read it again.

Indeed, even among the nobility one might well discover louts and skinflints who declare that we can get along without pastors and preachers from now on because we have it all in books and can learn everything for ourselves. So they cheerfully let parishes fall into wrack and ruin and bravely let pastors and preachers suffer and starve, that being the only proper treatment for such crazy Germans! Shameful people of this sort we Germans have to put up with.

As for myself, let me say this. I too am a doctor and a preacher. In fact, I am as educated and experienced as any of those who have all that nerve and brazen self-confidence. Yet I continue to do as a child does that is being taught the Catechism. Mornings, and when I otherwise have time, I read and recite word for word the Lord's Prayer, the Ten Commandments, the Creed, Psalms, etc. I must still read and study the Catechism daily, yet I cannot master it as I would like, but must remain a child and student of the Catechism. This I do gladly. But these dainty, choosy fellows want to win a doctorate above all doctorates and learn all there is to know in merely one rapid reading. So be it. But that is also a sure sign that they despise both their office and the souls of the people, yes, also God Himself and His Word. They need not

6

anticipate failing; they have already failed all too horribly. What they do need is to become children again and start learning their ABCs, which they falsely imagine they already long ago had under their belts.

I heartily beseech these lazy drones and arrogant saints that they would for God's sake get it into their heads that they really are not—repeat, really are not—such learned and lofty doctors of theology as they think. Though they suffer under the illusion that they know these parts of Christian doctrine contained in the Catechism far too well already, I implore them never to imagine that they have mastered them, or that they have even an adequate knowledge of them. Even if their knowledge of the Catechism truths were perfect (something that in this life is impossible), yet to read it daily and to make it the subject of one's thinking and conversation has all manner of practical results and brings fruitful rewards. In such reading, discussion, and meditation the Holy Spirit is present to supply always more light and new insights. Thus we come to relish and appreciate the Catechism better and better day by day. This bears out Christ's promise in Matthew 18:20, "Where two or three are gathered together in My name, there am I in the midst of them."

To occupy oneself with God's Word, talking about it and thinking about it, is also a most tremendous help against the devil, the world, the flesh, and all evil thoughts. Psalm 1:2 calls those blessed who meditate on the law of the Lord day and night. It is certain that you will be offering up no incense or candles more potent against the devil than by occupying yourself with God's commandments and words, by talking of them, by singing them, and by meditating on them. That, let me tell you, is the true holy water, the sign before which he flees and by which you can rout him.

Even if there were no other result or benefit, you should read the parts of Christian doctrine in the Catechism gladly and discuss, ponder, and practice them for this reason alone that thereby you can drive away the devil and evil thoughts. For he cannot stand to hear God's Word. The Word of God is not like some empty fiction, for example the tale about Dietrich von Bern [Theodoric], but as St. Paul says in Romans 1:16, it is "the power of God," the power, in fact, that flames out to blister the devil but to strengthen, comfort, and help us immeasurably.

Why should I go on? If I had to tell all the benefits and blessings that result when God's Word is at work, where would I find time enough and paper enough? The devil has been called the master of a thousand arts. What then shall we call God's Word, which routs and destroys this master of a thousand arts together with all his wiles and power? It must surely be the master of more than a hundred thousand arts. Are we, especially we who want to be pastors and preachers, frivolously to disdain this might, benefit, power, and success of the Word? If we do, we deserve not only to have our food cut off but also to be driven out by dogs and to be pelted with garbage as we go. Not only do we daily need God's Word as our daily spiritual bread, we also need to use it every day against the daily, unremitting ambushes and attacks of Satan with his thousand tricks.

If this is not enough admonition, there is also God's command. That in itself should be enough to impel us to read the Catechism daily. Deuteronomy 6:7-8 solemnly directs us always to meditate on God's precepts whether we are sitting, walking, standing, lying down, or getting up, and to keep them before our eyes and in our hands as a constant token and sign. It is certainly not for nothing that God requires and demands this so earnestly. He does so because He knows our danger and need. He knows the devil's constant and furious charges and attacks. Against these God wants to warn us, and He wants to arm us with good armor against Satan's "flaming darts" and to protect us with His good antidote against their evil poison. O what mad, senseless fools we are! Although we find that we must continue living and dwelling among such strong enemies as the devils are, yet we despise our weapons and armor, too lazy to give them a look or a thought.

What do you suppose those bored, arrogant saints are doing who don't like to read and learn the Catechism daily? What else than imagining they are much wiser than God Himself plus all His holy angels, prophets, apostles, and all Christians? God Himself, however, is not ashamed to teach the Christian doctrines every day. He knows of no better teachings than these; He always teaches these same ones; He presents nothing novel or different. And all His saints know of nothing better or different to be learned than this doctrine, and none of them ever finishes learning it all. Aren't we some splendid fellows, though, to imagine that if we have once learned it or heard it, we know it all and need to read or learn no more! Think of it! In one hour we can finish learning what God Himself cannot finish teaching, although He has been at

8

it from the beginning of the world and will continue to the end; the prophets, too, and all saints have been busy learning and yet have always remained pupils and must go on being pupils.

For this is certain that the person who knows the Ten Commandments perfectly knows the entire Scripture. In all cases and circumstances, he will be able to counsel, help, comfort, judge, and make decisions in both spiritual and temporal matters. He is qualified to sit in judgment upon all doctrines, classes of men, individual persons, laws, and whatever else is in the world.

Take the whole Book of Psalms. What else is it but reflections based on the First Commandment? Now, I know very well that those lazy lubbers, those arrogant fellows, do not understand a single psalm, let alone the entire Holy Scripture. Yet they put on that they know the Catechism, despising the book which is a brief summary and abstract of the entire Holy Scripture.

Once again, therefore, I beg all Christians, especially the pastors and preachers, not to try too soon to be doctors of theology and to imagine that they know it all. Inflated ideas, like new cloth, will shrink in the wash. Rather, let all Christians exercise themselves daily in the Catechism and put it into practice constantly. Let them guard themselves with greatest care and diligence against the poisonous infection of false security or self-delusion. Let them continue steadily reading, teaching, learning, thinking, and reflecting, never stopping until experience has made them absolutely certain that they have taught the devil to death and have grown more learned than God Himself and all His saints.

If they show such diligence, I can promise them—and they themselves will experience—that they will reap a harvest and that God will make fine persons of them, persons who in time will make the excellent confession that the longer they use the Catechism, the less they know of it and the more they have to learn. Then, because they are hungry and thirsty for the Word, that which now in their bloated, surfeited state they do not even care to smell will first begin to taste really good to them. To that end may God grant His grace. Amen.

# Preface [1528]

This presentation has been undertaken for the instruction of children and the theologically unlearned. It is in a form that in ancient Greek was called a "catechism," that is, instruction for children. It contains the minimum of knowledge a Christian should have. Whoever lacks this knowledge cannot be counted among Christians nor be admitted to the sacraments. Here the situation is the same as when a craftsman who does not know the rules and techniques of his craft is regarded as incompetent and is rejected. Accordingly, one should thoroughly instruct young people in the various teachings of the Catechism or the children's sermons and diligently drill them in putting them into practice.

It is therefore the duty of every family head to examine his children and household members at least once a week to see what they have learned of the Catechism. If they do not know it, he should insist earnestly that they keep working at it. It still happens every day, as I well remember it happening in the past, that old people who were and are totally ignorant of these basics of Christianity nevertheless come to Baptism and the Sacrament of the Altar and partake of all Christian rights and privileges, even though those who come to a sacrament certainly ought to have a better knowledge of and a fuller insight into all Christian doctrine than children beginning school. In the case of the common people, however, we can be satisfied if they learn the three main parts: the Ten Commandments, the Creed, and the Lord's Prayer, maintained in Christendom since ancient times but rarely taught and applied correctly, so that Christians young and old who want to be Christians in fact as well as in name may be at home in these teachings and put them into live practice.

## I. God's Ten Commandments

1. Thou shalt have no other gods before Me.
2. Thou shalt not take the name of the Lord, thy God, in vain.
3. Thou shalt sanctify the holy day.
4. Thou shalt honor thy father and thy mother, that it may be well with thee, and thou mayest live long on the earth.
5. Thou shalt not kill.
6. Thou shalt not commit adultery.
7. Thou shalt not steal.
8. Thou shalt not bear false witness against thy neighbor.
9. Thou shalt not covet thy neighbor's house.
10. Thou shalt not covet thy neighbor's wife, nor his manservant, nor his maidservant, nor his cattle, nor anything that is thy neighbor's.

## II. The Chief Articles of Our Faith

I believe in God the Father Almighty, Maker of heaven and earth.

And in Jesus Christ, His only Son, our Lord, who was conceived by the Holy Ghost, born of the Virgin Mary, suffered under Pontius Pilate, was crucified, dead, and buried; He descended into hell; the third day He rose again from the dead; He ascended into heaven and sitteth on the right hand of God the Father Almighty; from thence He shall come to judge the quick and the dead.

I believe in the Holy Ghost; the holy Christian church, the communion of saints; the forgiveness of sins; the resurrection of the body; and the life everlasting. Amen.

## III. The Our Father, the Prayer That Christ Taught Us

Our Father who art in heaven, Hallowed be Thy name; Thy kingdom come; Thy will be done on earth as it is in heaven; Give us this day our daily bread; And forgive us our trespasses, as we forgive those who trespass against us; And lead us not into temptation; But deliver us from evil. For Thine is the kingdom and the power and the glory forever and ever. Amen.

These are the most necessary parts of the Christian teaching, and they must first be learned well enough to repeat them word for word. We should teach our children to repeat them regularly in the morning when they get up, during the day at mealtimes, and in the evening when they go to bed. They should be given food and drink only after they have repeated them. Every father has this same responsibility toward members of the household, servants, and maids; if they do not know and will not learn these things, he should dismiss them. In no case should a person be tolerated who is so loutish and unruly that he will not learn these three parts in which all that Scripture contains is briefly and plainly summarized. The dear ancient fathers, or the apostles, as the case may be, have here arranged a digest of the doctrine, life, wisdom, and insight of Christians, everything that animates their speech, conduct, and concern.

Now, when these three parts are grasped, the proper next step is to know what to say about the sacraments that Christ Himself instituted, Baptism and the holy body and blood of Christ, according to the texts of Matthew and Mark at the end of their Gospels where they record Christ's last words to His disciples as He sent them forth.

### Baptism

"Go ye . . . and teach all nations, baptizing them in the name of the Father and of the Son and of the Holy Ghost" (Matthew 28:19). "He that believeth and is baptized shall be saved; but he that believeth not shall be damned" (Mark 16:16).

This much is enough for an ordinary person to know from Scripture concerning Baptism. The other sacrament may be presented similarly in short, plain words, as for example in the passage from St. Paul.

### The Sacrament of the Altar

"Our Lord Jesus Christ on the night when He was betrayed took bread, gave thanks, and broke it and gave it to His disciples, saying, 'Take and eat; this is My body, which is given for you. This do in remembrance of Me.'

"In the same manner also He took the cup, after supper, saying, 'This cup is the new testament in My blood, which is shed for you for the forgiveness of sins. Do this, as often as you drink it, in remembrance of Me'" (1 Corinthians 11:23-25).

Thus we have a total of five parts covering the whole Christian teaching. These we should work with constantly and require the young to know and recite them word for word. Do not depend on young folk learning and remembering the Christian teachings from sermons alone. And when they have learned these five parts well, then you may also assign

a few psalms, or hymns based on the Catechism topics
will supplement and reinforce their knowledge. Thus
youth will be brought further into the Scriptures and v
make daily progress. It is not enough, however, for them
simply to learn the words and to be able to recite the chief
parts of Christian doctrine. The young people should also
attend preaching services, especially when the pastor has
scheduled sermons on the Catechism, so that they hear it
explained and learn to understand the meaning of each part.
Then they will be able to repeat what they have heard and
give good answers when questioned, and the preaching will
not be without benefits and results. The reason why we
carefully make a point of preaching often on the Catechism is
to impress it on our youth, not in high-toned, sophisticated
language, but briefly and in very plain terms, so that it may
reach their hearts and remain fixed in their minds.

We shall accordingly take up the indicated parts of
Christian teaching one by one, using the very plainest terms
to say what is necessary.

### First Part

## THE TEN COMMANDMENTS

### The First Commandment

*"Thou shalt have no other gods before Me."*

To rephrase this: "You are to regard Me alone as your
God." What does that mean? How is one to understand it?
What is it to *have* a god? Or, what is one's god?

Answer: To whatever we look for any good thing and for
refuge in every need, that is what is meant by "god." To *have*
a god is nothing else than to trust and believe in him from the
heart. As I have often said, it is the trust and faith of the heart,
nothing else, that make both God and an idol. If your faith and
confidence are of the right kind, then your God is the true
God. If, on the other hand, your trust is false, if it is
misdirected, then you do not have the true God. For these two,
faith and God, belong together. To whatever you give your
heart and entrust your being, that, I say, is really your God.

The point of this commandment, therefore, is to require
that kind of true faith and confidence of the heart that is
directed toward the one true God and clings to Him alone. The
meaning is: "See to it that you let Me alone be your God, and
never look about for another." In other words: "Look to Me for

any good thing that you lack; come to Me for it. And whenever you suffer misfortune and distress, reach out to Me and hold on to Me. I, and I alone, will satisfy your need and help you in every trouble. Only do not ever let your heart cling to or depend on anything or anybody else."

In order that this meaning may be grasped and kept in mind, I must highlight it, a bit crudely perhaps, by pointing to some common examples of the opposite kind of behavior. Many a person imagines that he has God and everything he needs, provided he has money and property. He relies upon these, boasts about them, and feels so immovably secure that he cares about no one. But look, he too has a god, named mammon, that is the money and property to which he has given his whole heart. Mammon is the world's favorite idol. One who has money and property has a sense of security and feels as happy and fearless as if he were sitting in the middle of paradise. On the other hand, one who has nothing is as insecure and anxiety-ridden as if he had never heard of God. Very few can be found who keep a cheerful spirit and neither fret nor complain when they are without mammon. The desire for riches sticks glued to our nature right up to the grave.

Similarly, one who congratulates himself on his great learning, intelligence, power, special advantages, family connections, and honor and trusts in them also has a god, only not the one true God. The evidence for this appears when people are arrogant, secure, and proud because of such possessions, but desperate when they lack them or lose them. I repeat, to have a god means to have something on which one's heart depends entirely.

See, for instance, how blindly we used to carry on under the papacy. If someone had a toothache, he would fast in honor of Saint Apollonia; if he was afraid of loss by fire, he looked to Saint Lawrence for protection; if he feared the plague, he made vows to Saint Sebastian or Saint Roch, not to mention other abominations, everyone choosing his own saint to worship and call upon in times of trouble. Here also belong those who go wildly overboard and make a pact with the devil so that he will give them plenty of money, help them to a lover, protect their cattle, restore their lost property, etc., as sorcerers and black magicians do. For all these fix their heart's reliance elsewhere than upon the true God, neither expecting nor seeking any good thing from Him.

So now you can easily understand what it is and how

much it is that this commandment requires. It requires that man's whole heart and all his confidence be given to God alone and no one else. For you can well realize that to have God is not a matter of taking and grasping Him with one's fingers or putting Him into a wallet or shutting Him up in a strong box. Laying hold of God means that our heart embraces Him and clings to Him. But to cling to Him with the heart is nothing else than to place ourselves completely into His hands. He wants to turn us away from everything else, and to draw us to Himself, because He is the only eternal good It is as if He were to say: Everything that you formerly sought to find in the saints or which you confidently expected from mammon or from whatever else, look to Me for all that; recognize Me as the One who wants to help you and is anxious richly to lavish upon you every good thing.

Look, there you have the true worship and service of God, the kind that pleases Him and which He also commands on pain of everlasting wrath. True worship and service of God takes place when your heart directs all its trust and confidence only toward God and does not let itself be torn away from Him; it consists in risking everything on earth for Him and abandoning it all for His sake. You can easily judge how, in contrast to this, the world practices nothing but false worship and idolatry. There has never been a people so wicked that it did not institute and practice some sort of worship. Everyone has set up for himself some particular god to which he looks for benefits, help, and comfort.

The pagans, for example, who placed their trust in power and rulership raised Jupiter to the position of supreme god; others whose aim was riches, success, pleasure, and the "good life" worshiped Hercules, Mercury, Venus, and similar gods, while pregnant women worshiped Diana or Lucina, and so on. Everyone chose for himself that deity to which his heart was drawn. Actually, then, also all the pagans understand that to have a god means to trust and believe. The trouble is that their trust is false, misdirected, not built on the one God, apart from whom there truly is no god in heaven or on earth. Thus the heathen actually turn their own fictitious notions and dreams about God into idols and put their trust in what is absolutely nothing. So it is with all idolatry. For idolatry does not consist simply in setting up an image and worshiping it; it takes place primarily in the heart, which looks elsewhere than to the one God, seeks help and comfort in created things, in saints, or in devils. Idolaters in their

15

hearts neither embrace God nor expect Him even to be kind enough to desire to help them; nor do they believe that all good things they experience come to them from God.

Besides this there is also that false worship, that height of idolatry, which we used to practice, which is still prevalent in the world, and upon which all the religious orders are founded. It involves only the conscience of those who seek comfort and salvation in their own works and presume to capture heaven by putting God under the pressure of an obligation. They keep a record of how often they have made donations, fasted, celebrated mass, etc. They rely on such things and dwell upon them, unwilling to receive anything from God as a gift. Instead, they wish to earn everything themselves or merit it by works beyond the call of duty. This is exactly as if God had to stand under obligation to us, with Him as our debtor, we as the lenders. What is this but turning God into an idol, into a plaster image, while the worshiper actually is setting himself up as his own god. But what I have said here is a little too subtle for the young and is not meant for them.

However, in order that they may take careful note of the meaning of this commandment and remember it, the un-schooled should be told this: We are to trust in God alone, look to Him, and expect to receive nothing but good things from Him; He it is who gives us body, life, food, drink, nourishment, health, protection, peace, and everything we need by way of temporal and eternal blessings; He it is who in addition guards us against misfortune and when something does go against us helps and delivers us. Thus, as I have said often enough, God alone is the One from whom we receive whatever is good and who delivers us from whatever is evil. For this reason we from ancient times call God by a more precise and fitting name, in my opinion, than other languages do, a name that comes from the little word "good" and thus indicates that God is the eternal fountain overflowing with pure goodness and that everything that both in name and in fact is good flows forth from Him.

For even if many of the good things we experience come to us through people, we nevertheless receive them all from God as things that reach us according to His command and ordinance. For our parents and all who have authority over us, indeed all who stand in the relation of neighbor to us, have been commanded to do all manner of good things for us. These things we therefore receive not from them but from

16

God through them. God's creatures are merely the hands, channels, and means through which He bestows all good things. For example, He gives breasts and milk to a mother to offer them to her infant; and He gives grain and all kinds of fruits of the earth for food, things that no creature could produce independently. Therefore no one should presume either to take or give anything except as commanded by God, recognizing all these things as God's gifts and thanking Him for them, as this commandment requires. Conversely, we are not to disdain this way of getting good things from God through His creatures, nor are we arrogantly to seek other ways and means to obtain them than those He commanded; to do so would be not to receive them from God as His gifts but to look for them in ourselves.

So let each one for himself above all things see to it that he values this commandment far beyond everything else and that he does not toss it to the winds. Question and explore your own heart thoroughly, and you will find out if it embraces God alone or not. Do you have it in your heart to expect nothing but good things from God, especially when you are in trouble and in need? And does your heart in addition give up and forsake everything that is not God? Then you have the one true God. On the other hand, is your heart attached to and does it rely on something else, from which you hope to receive more good and more help than from God? And when things go wrong, do you, instead of fleeing to Him, flee from Him? Then you have another god, a false god.

So that one may see that God does not want this commandment to be thrown to the winds but that He will keep strict watch over it, He has attached to it first a terrible threat and then a beautifully reassuring promise. These also we should thoroughly drill, impressing them upon young people so that they take them to heart and remember them.

### Explanation of the Appendix to the First Commandment

"For I the Lord your God am a jealous God, visiting the iniquity of the fathers upon the children to the third and fourth generation of those who hate Me, but showing steadfast love to thousands of those who love Me and keep My commandments" (Exodus 20:5b-6).

Although, as we shall hear, these words apply to all the commandments, yet they are attached here to this one because the most important thing for a person is to have the

17

right kind of head. For when the head is right, then the entire life, too, must be right, and vice versa. So, then, learn from these words how angry God is with those who rely on anything other than Himself, and again, how kind and gracious He is to those who trust and believe in Him alone with all their heart. His wrath will not let up until the fourth generation; on the other hand, His kindness and goodness extend over many thousands. He intends that people should not go on so cocksure, trusting to luck like the clods who think it does not matter much how they live. He is not the kind of God who lets it go unpunished when people turn away from Him, and His anger will not stop before the fourth generation until they have been totally uprooted. He intends to be reverently feared and not despised.

This He has proved in all of recorded history, as Scripture abundantly demonstrates. Daily experience is still able to teach us the same thing. From the beginning He has continued thoroughly to stamp out all idolatries and on their account He has destroyed both pagans and Jews. Similarly in our day He brings down all false worship, so that ultimately all those who continue in it must perish. Today there are certain proud, powerful, rich maggots, defiantly boastful of their mammon and not caring whether God smiles or frowns, who confidently expect to outlast the tempest of God's wrath. But they will not succeed. Before they know it, they will be dashed to pieces and perish together with all that they trusted in, just as all the others went under who thought they were much too secure and powerful for that to happen to them.

Because God stands aside for a while without shaking their security, some imagine that their attitudes and ways matter nothing to Him or that He overlooks them. It is precisely because they are such knuckleheads that He needs to strike hard and punish without letup down to their children's children in order that everyone may be staggered by it and see that it is no joking matter with Him. For these are also the ones He means when He refers to those "who hate Me," that is, those who persist in their defiance and pride. They refuse to hear what is preached or spoken to them. If one rebukes them in order to bring them to their senses and to an amendment of life before their punishment strikes, they become so furious and foolish that they well deserve the descending wrath. We see this happening every day in the case of bishops and princes.

Awesome as these threats are, much mightier is the

comfort of the promise that for those who cling to God alone, His mercy is certain—sheer goodness and blessing to be shown not only to them but also to their children to a thousand, yes, to many thousands of generations. The divine Majesty comes to us with so gracious an offer, He so heartily invites us to take it, and He attaches so rich a promise to it that, if we desire every good for time and eternity, all this surely ought to move and drive us to fix our hearts in total trust upon God.

Therefore let everyone genuinely take this in and not regard it as mere human opinion. For it brings you either eternal blessing, happiness, and salvation, or eternal wrath, misery, and heartache. What more could you wish or ask for than this gracious promise of God that He will be yours, together with every blessing, and that He will help and protect you in every need? Sad to say, the world believes none of this nor takes it to be the Word of God. For the world sees that those who do trust in God and not in mammon suffer cares and troubles and are oppressed and set upon by the devil until they have neither money, status, nor honor, and even barely escape with their lives. On the other hand, in the eyes of the world those who serve mammon have power, prestige, honor, and wealth, and every kind of security. In the face of this seeming contradiction, we must therefore lay firm hold on these words and know that they neither lie nor deceive but will in the end prove true.

Think about it yourself, or make inquiries, and then tell me: What did those finally accomplish who directed all their efforts and energies toward raking together a lot of property and money? You will find that they either wasted their effort and toil, or, even if they piled up great wealth, yet it all turned to dust and was blown away. They themselves had no joy in their possessions, which afterward did not even last to the third generation. You will find plenty of examples for this in all history books; old, experienced people will tell you the same. Be sure to take note and pay attention to this. Saul was a great king, a man chosen by God and pious. But once he was securely seated on his throne, he let his heart turn away from God and set his trust in his crown and power. As a result he inevitably perished together with all that he had, so that not one of his children remained. David, by contrast, was a poor, despised man, shunned and driven out, his life nowhere safe; yet he inevitably survived persecution by Saul and became king. For these words must stand and be proven true because

God cannot lie or deceive; leave it up to the world to deceive you with fair appearances, which may indeed last a while but ultimately come to nothing.

So let us learn the First Commandment well and realize that God intends to put up with no arrogant self-reliance or trust in anything else than Himself, and that He requires nothing more demanding of us than heartfelt trust in Him for every blessing. Then we will go straight forward on the right course, using all of God's gifts the way a shoemaker uses his needle, awl, and thread for his work and then lays them aside; or as a guest at an inn uses the accommodations, food, and bed merely for his temporal needs. Let each person make use of these good things according to God's order for his particular station and be sure to allow none of them to become his lord or idol.

Let this be enough about the First Commandment, which needed to be explained thoroughly and at length because, as was stated above, if the heart is in a right relationship with God and this commandment is kept, then all the other commandments will follow of themselves.

### The Second Commandment

*"Thou shalt not take the name of the Lord, thy God, in vain."*

As the First Commandment inwardly instructs the heart and teaches faith, so this commandment leads outward, and directs the speech of lips and tongue into a right relationship to God. The first things that break forth out of the heart and come into the open are words. As I have taught above regarding the way to answer the question, "What does it mean to have a god?" so you must learn to grasp also the meaning of this commandment in its straightforward sense and apply it to your own self. If, now, someone asks, "How do you understand the Second Commandment?" or "What does it mean to misuse God's name or to use it in vain?" then you should answer very briefly: "Misusing God's name is when one speaks the name of the Lord God, in whatever manner that may be, in order to support lies or any kind of wrong." Thus this commandment forbids the falseness of appealing to God's name or taking it upon our lips to support a statement when the heart knows or should know that the facts are otherwise than stated. An example of this is when in court people take oaths and yet one side lies against the other. One cannot more grievously misuse God's name than by using it

20

for purposes of falsehood and deception. Let this explanation stand as the sense of the commandment expressed in easiest colloquial terms.

From this everyone can easily figure out for himself when and in what a variety of ways God's name is misused, although it is impossible to list them all. But here is a brief rundown. First to meet the eye are the misuses of God's name in worldly business and in matters involving money, property, and prestige, whether publicly in court or in the marketplace or elsewhere, as when a person swears a false oath by God's name or backs up a falsehood with a reference to his conscience. This kind of thing is especially common in marriage matters when two persons become secretly engaged and later deny it under oath.

The greatest misuse, however, occurs in spiritual matters involving the conscience, when false preachers arise and parade their lying trumpery as the Word of God.

Note well that all this is a matter of pluming oneself with God's name in order to polish one's image or to put on a show of right, whether in secular dealings or in some lofty and rarified point of Christian faith and doctrine. Blasphemers, too, are to be counted among the liars, and not only the totally shameless ones whom everyone recognizes, who do not hesitate to drag down the name of God (they are material for the hangman's school, not ours), but also those who publicly run down God's truth and Word and ascribe it to the devil. There is no need to say any more about this.

Now let us learn and take to heart the great importance of this commandment, so that we may diligently avoid and shun all the various misuses of the sacred name, the gravest sins that can be outwardly committed. For lying and deceiving are in themselves grave sins, but they become much more serious when one tries to justify oneself by dragging in God's name to back them up, using His name as a cover-up for evil, with the result that the original lie is doubled, yes, compounded into a multitude of lies.

Therefore God has attached also to this commandment a solemn threat, which is that "the Lord will not regard as guiltless anyone who uses His name without a good purpose." This means that nobody will get by with it or remain unpunished for it. For just as certainly as God will let no one escape punishment who in his heart turns away from Him, so certainly will He not tolerate the use of His name as a front for lying. Sad to say, it is a common disease of epidemic proportions that as many use God's name for lying and all manner of evil as there are few who trust in God alone with their whole heart.

What a terribly splendid virtue in our nature it is that if we have done something wrong, we like to cover up and disguise our disgrace so that nobody might see it or know about it! There is nobody so utterly brazen that he would proudly display before everyone the wickedness he has committed. We all prefer to do it secretly without having others become aware of it. If someone is taken to task for his wrongdoing, then God and His name have to be dragged in to make the rascality seem righteous and the disgraceful thing seem honorable. This is the usual way of the world. It is like a great deluge flooding every land. Therefore we have as our reward the very things which our behavior invites and deserves: epidemics, war, food shortages, fires, floods, wayward wives and children and workers, and all manner of evil. Where else could so much misery come from? It is only the special mercy of God that the earth in spite of all this still supports and sustains us.

Therefore above all else we should strictly require and train our young people to hold this commandment and all the others in high regard. Whenever they transgress, we must at once be after them with the rod, hold this commandment before them, and constantly impress it on them, so that they may be brought up not just with punishments but in the reverence and fear of God.

You now understand what it means to misuse the name of God. To repeat it very briefly, it means to use God's name as a cover for lying—for presenting something as true though it is not—or for cursing, swearing, engaging in occult practices, in short, for wickedness of any kind.

In addition, you must know how to use the divine name rightly. When God says, "You are not to use God's name in vain," He therewith also gives us to understand that we are to use His name and use it properly. For His name is revealed and given to us precisely in order that it should be used for beneficial purposes. Since we are forbidden to use God's name for falsehood or wrongdoing, it follows of itself that we are conversely commanded to use it in support of the truth and all that is good. Examples of this are: swearing rightful oaths when necessary and required, also teaching the true doctrine, calling on His name in times of trouble, praising and thanking Him in good days, and the like. All of which is summarized in Psalm 50:15: "Call upon Me in the day of trouble; I will deliver you, and you shall glorify Me." All this is what is meant by calling upon God's name and using it reverently in the service of the truth. Thus God's name is hallowed, as according to the Lord's Prayer it should be.

There you have the essentials of the entire commandment explained. With this understanding of the commandment, a question over which many teachers have agonized is easily solved, namely, why swearing oaths is forbidden in the Gospel, although Christ, St. Paul, and other saints often took oaths. The explanation is briefly this: one is not to swear in support of evil (that is, to a falsehood) or when it is not necessary or not beneficial; but in a good cause and for the benefit of one's neighbor one should swear. This kind of swearing is a really good work through which God is honored, truth and justice are established, lies are refuted, people are reconciled, obedience is rendered, and strife is ended. For here God Himself steps in to separate right from wrong, good from evil. If one of the contending parties swears falsely, the sentence goes against him and he will not escape punishment. Even if his punishment is long delayed, yet in the end nothing will succeed for him; everything that he won by his false oath will slip from his hands and he will never happily enjoy it. This I have observed in many cases of persons who under oath denied their matrimonial vows and thereafter never enjoyed a happy hour or a healthful day and came to miserable ruin of body, soul, and property.

Therefore I urge and admonish, as before, that by means of warnings and threats, checks and penalties children should be trained early to shun falsehood and especially to avoid bringing in God's name to support it. For nothing good will come of it if one lets them carry on as they please. It is clear that the world today is more wicked than it ever was. There is no control, no obedience, no sincerity, no faith—nothing but insolent, disorderly people, whom neither teaching nor punishment can help. All this is the wrath and punishment of God upon such wanton contempt of this commandment.

On the other hand, we should also constantly urge and encourage children to honor God's name and to have it constantly on their lips no matter what they meet up with in their experience. For truly to honor God's name means looking to Him and praying to Him for all consolation; as we have heard before, first the heart by faith gives God the honor

23

that belongs to Him, and then the lips do so by confessing His name.

This is also a blessed, useful practice, and a powerfully effective one, against the devil, who is always lurking around trying to bring us into sin and shame, misery and trouble. He has a very strong distaste for the name of God and cannot stay around long where anyone utters and calls upon God's name from the heart. Many a frightful, horrible disaster would strike us if God did not preserve us at our calling upon His name. I myself have personally tried it out and have found that often some great sudden accident was averted when I called upon God's name. To spite the devil we should, I say, always have God's name on our lips, so that our foe cannot harm us as he would like to do.

It also helps toward this end if one makes it a habit to commit oneself—with soul and body, wife, children, household, and whatever is ours—daily to God's care for every possible eventuality. Thus our custom of praying before and after meals and of having morning and evening prayers arose and continued. In the same way the children's custom originated of making the sign of the cross and saying, "Lord God, save us," "Help, dear Lord Christ," or the like, when they see or hear something frightful and horrible. So, too, on the other hand, when something good—no matter how light—happens unexpectedly to someone, he should say, "God be thanked and praised," "God did this for me," etc., just as formerly children were trained to fast and to pray to St. Nicholas and other saints. Using God's name as here indicated would be more acceptable and pleasing to Him than any monastic life, even the "holiness" of the Carthusian Order.

Notice that by means of such childlike and playful methods we may bring up our youth to reverence and honor God so that they constantly observe and put into practice the First and Second Commandments. Thus something good could take root, sprout, and bear fruit, so that the young would develop into the kind of adults of whom the whole country may be proud. That would be the right way to bring up children as long as one uses kind and agreeable methods. Those who can only be forced by means of rods and blows come to no good; for even if they seem to make improvement, they will stay good only as long as the rod is on their backs.

Proper training, however, takes such root in their hearts that they reverence God rather than fear switches and blows.

I am speaking in simple terms for the sake of the young, so that it may finally sink in. For when we preach to children, we must speak their language. Thus we prevent the misuse of God's name and teach its proper use, which consists not merely in words but also in action and life style. We want children to know that God is heartily pleased with our right use of His name and that He will richly reward it, just as He will punish terribly its every misuse.

## The Third Commandment

*"Thou shalt sanctify the holy day."*

Our word "holy day" or "holiday" is analogous to the Hebrew "Sabbath," which really implies celebration, for it means to rest, that is to cease from labor; our usual expressions for having time off from work are "having a holiday" or "observing a holy day." In the Old Testament God set apart the seventh day and instituted it to be a day of rest, and He commanded it to be kept holy above every other day. As far as the external observance of the day is concerned, this commandment applied only to the Jews. They were to desist from heavy work and to rest on this day for the refreshment both of man and beast, lest constant work exhaust them. Later, however, they took this commandment much too narrowly and crudely misused it; they went so far as to blaspheme Christ Himself and, as we read in the Gospels, found it intolerable that He did on the Sabbath what they themselves would have done. They acted as if the commandment could be fulfilled by avoiding every kind of manual labor whatever. This was not its intention, but, as we shall hear, it meant that the holy day or day of rest should be kept sacred.

According to its literal and external sense, therefore, this commandment is of no concern to us Christians. For in this sense it is a totally external thing like the other Old Testament regulations that are bound to specific customs, persons, times, and places, all of which have been made optional through Christ.

But let us formulate for everyday folk the Christian sense of what God requires in this commandment. Note that we observe holy days not for the welfare of intelligent and learned Christians, for these do not need them. We observe them, first, for the sake of the body and its needs. Nature is insistent in teaching that the common people—hired men and domestic servants who have attended to their work and occupation all week long—should withdraw from work for a day of rest and refreshment. Second, we observe holy days especially in order that people may have the time and opportunity, otherwise unavailable, for participation in divine worship, for coming together to hear and to work with the Word of God and to praise God by song and prayer.

This command is not, I say, tied to specific times as with the Jews, for whom this or that specific day was prescribed. For no day is in itself better than another. Actually, one should worship daily. But since people for the most part cannot do this, it is necessary to set aside at least one day in the week for it. Since traditionally Sunday has been appointed as the day of worship, we should stay with it, so that there may be a uniform order and so that no one brings about disorder through unnecessary change.

The plain sense of this commandment, then, is that since we observe holidays in any case, we should use them for learning God's Word. For the sake of young people and the neglected masses, the ministry of the Word should be the special concern of this day. However, the observance of the day of rest should not be so narrowly restrictive that it forbids incidental and unavoidable work.

If, then, someone asks the meaning of "Thou shalt sanctify the holy day," then reply, "To sanctify the holy day means to keep it holy." But what is "keeping it holy"? It is nothing else than to reserve it for holy words, holy works, and holy living. For the day as such requires no sanctifying, for it was created holy in itself. But God wants it to be holy for you. It is through you that it becomes holy on unholy depending on whether what you do on that day is holy or unholy.

How, then, is such sanctifying accomplished? Not by sitting cozily in a corner and avoiding hard work, nor by decking oneself with flower garlands and putting on one's best clothes, but, as stated, by our being occupied with God's Word and putting it into practice.

Indeed, we Christians ought to observe an ongoing holy day and be totally involved with holy things, that is, daily occupy ourselves with God's Word, carrying it in our hearts and on our lips. But because not everyone has the time and leisure for this, we must, as was pointed out, use several hours during the week for the young and at least one day of the week for the whole community, solely in order to focus on these things, especially on the Ten Commandments, the Creed, and the Lord's Prayer. In that way our entire life and being will be under the direction of God's Word. Be the time slot what it may, wherever there are such activities and exercises, there a true holy day is kept. Wherever these are lacking, it cannot be called a Christian holy day. For non-Christians can take days for rest and idleness as well as anyone, and so can the whole swarm of clerics in our day who stand in church every day singing and tinkling bells without sanctifying the holy day at all because they neither preach nor practice God's Word but actually teach and live contrary to it.

For the Word of God is the supreme object of veneration, in fact, it is the only sacred object of veneration that we Christians recognize and possess. For even if we gathered into one heap the bones of all the saints together with all holy, consecrated vestments, all these would not help us in the least. They are all dead things and cannot sanctify any one. The treasure that sanctifies all things is the Word of God, by which the saints themselves were all sanctified. In whatever hour one uses, preaches, hears, reads, or thinks about God's Word, it sanctifies the person, his day, and his work, not because of the external act, but because of the Word that makes saints of us all. Therefore I keep repeating that if our life and labor are to be God-pleasing or holy, they must be conducted in the light of the Word of God. Where that happens, there the Third Commandment is being observed according to its full intent.

By contrast, any life-style or labor carried on apart from God's Word is unholy in the eyes of God, no matter how much it may seem to shine and glisten; this holds true even if it were totally festooned with holy relics, as are the so-called spiritual orders, which do not know God's Word and seek their holiness in their own works.

Notice, therefore, that the vital thrust of this commandment is not a matter of physical rest but of sanctifying, so that this day may have its own particular holy work. Other labors and occupations cannot properly be called holy work unless the person first is holy. But here that work is to be done which makes the person himself holy; and, as we have heard, people are made holy only through God's Word. Places, times, persons, and the entire external order of worship have been instituted and appointed in order that God's Word may publicly do this work of making people holy.

So much depends on God's Word that without it no holy

27

day is sanctified. We should therefore realize that God wants this commandment to be strictly kept and will punish all who despise God's Word and do not want to hear or learn it, especially at the times set aside for it.

Those who grossly misuse and desecrate the holy day, those, for example, who neglect God's Word because of greed or frivolity or who laze about in taprooms, drinking and stuffing themselves like swine, are not the only ones who violate this commandment. It is transgressed also by that other crowd who listen to God's Word as to some entertainment and come to the preaching service merely by the force of habit and leave again with as little understanding of the Word at the end of the year as at the beginning. People used to think that Sunday had been properly observed if one had heard a mass or a Gospel reading; nobody asked for God's Word, in fact nobody taught it. Today we do have God's Word, but we nevertheless fail to eliminate its misuse; we let ourselves be preached to and admonished, but we listen without earnestness and serious concern.

Bear in mind, therefore, that you must be concerned not merely to listen to God's Word but also to learn it and remember it. Do not imagine that this is optional or that it matters little one way or the other. Realize instead that here is God's command and that He will call upon you to give an account of how you heard, learned, and honored His Word.

Also those conceited individuals are to be similarly rebuked who when they have heard one or two sermons turn up their noses at any more, imagining that they now know it all and need no more instruction. That is precisely the sin that has hitherto been counted among the deadly sins and was called acedia, that is, apathy or indifference, a malignant, destructive plague with which the devil bewitches and deceives in order to take us unawares and steal the Word of God away from us again.

Be sure to get this: even if you knew the Word of God through and through and had mastered everything, yet all your days are spent in the devil's territory, and he rests neither day nor night from stealthily trying to sneak up and kindle in your heart unfaith and evil thoughts against all the commandments. Therefore you must at all times have the Word of God in your heart, on your lips, and in your ears. But where the heart remains unmoved and the Word does not resound, there the devil breaks in and does his damage before one realizes it. On the other hand, when we sincerely ponder, hear, and apply the Word, it has such power that its fruit never fails. The Word always awakens new understandings, new delights, and a new spirit of devotion, and it constantly cleanses our heart and our thinking. For here are not limp and lifeless words, but words that are alive and move to living action. And even if no other benefit or need drove us into the Word, everyone should be impelled by the fact that our using the Word shows the devil the door and drives him away, besides the fact that it fulfills this commandment and pleases God more than the glitter of any work of hypocrisy.

### The Fourth Commandment

So far we have learned the first three commandments, in which the reference is to God. First, throughout our lives we are wholeheartedly to trust, reverence, and love Him. Second, we are not to misuse His name for lying or for anything that is wrong, but we are to use it only for the praise of God and the welfare and salvation of our neighbors and ourselves. Third, on holy days and days of rest we are to concern ourselves with and be actively involved in the use of the Word of God, so that our conduct and life may be under its direction. Now there follow the other seven commandments, which have reference to our neighbor. The first and greatest among these is:

*"Thou shalt honor thy father and thy mother."*

In preference to all the other lesser stations of life, God has given special recognition to fatherhood and motherhood by commanding not merely that we should love our parents but also that we should honor them. As regards brothers, sisters, and neighbors in general, He commands nothing higher than to love them. Thus He distinguishes father and mother from all other persons on earth, chooses them, and sets them next to Himself. For to honor is a much higher thing than to love, for honor includes not only love but also respect, humility, and awe, directed, one might say, toward a hidden majesty of theirs. The commandment requires not only that we address them in an affectionate and respectful manner but above all that we show by our emotional and physical behavior that we think highly of them and regard them as occupying the highest place in our lives next to God. For if we from the heart are genuinely to honor someone, then we must have him standing truly high and great in our estimation.

Young people must therefore have it impressed upon them

29

that they should look up to their parents as representatives of God and bear in mind that, however humble, poor, infirm, or eccentric they may be, our father and mother are nevertheless God's gifts to us. They are not to be robbed of their honor because of any peculiarities or failings. We are not to be influenced by their persons, whatever these may be, but rather by the will of God, who has created and ordained their parental relationship to us. In other respects we are all, it is true, equal in the eyes of God, but in our relationships with each other we cannot do without inequalities and regular distinctions of this sort. God therefore commands that these be observed and that you be obedient to me as your father and recognize my authority over you.

First, then, learn what it means to honor parents as this commandment requires. It means that you are above all to prize and value them as earth's greatest treasure. Next, in speaking to them you are to behave respectfully, never address them in a rude, taunting, or challenging matter, but give in to them and hold your tongue even when they go too far. Third, by means of your actions, both physical and financial, you are to show them honor by serving them, helping them, and providing for them when they are old, sick, infirm, or poor. All this you should do not only willingly but also with humility and respect as one who is under the scrutiny of God. For one whose heart has the right attitude toward parents will not let them suffer need or go hungry but will put them ahead of himself, stand at their side, and share with them everything he has to the best of his ability.

Furthermore, notice carefully what a great, good, and holy work is here assigned to children. Too bad that it is so thoroughly despised, neglected, and thrown to the winds. Nobody recognizes it as a command of God, as a sacred, divine Word and directive. For if we had considered it as such, then everyone could have deduced that men who lived according to these words had to be holy. Then there would not have been any need for setting up monasticism or spiritual orders. Every child would then have stayed with this commandment and would have been able in his conscience to face God and say, "If I am to do good and holy deeds, then I know of none better than to show every honor and obedience to my parents. For what God commands must be very much nobler than anything which we ourselves might invent. And because no greater or better teacher can be found than God, there can obviously be no better teaching than that which comes from Him. Now, His teaching is rich in directions about what we should do if we wish to be active in truly good works; and by commanding us to do them, He shows that they really please Him. Since here we have a command of God, the very best that His wisdon can devise, therefore I will never be able to improve upon it."

See, this is the way we might have had godly children, properly taught, brought up to be a blessing, and living at home in obedience and service to their parents. That would have been a good thing and a joy to behold. But people did not feel obligated to display God's commandment in all its splendor. Instead, they neglected it and brushed lightly over it. Thus children were not able to think it through but only stared openmouthed at the ensemble of notions which, without looking to God for His approval, we threw together in its place.

Let us for God's sake finally learn that young folk should put everything else aside and concentrate first of all on this commandment. If they wish to serve God with really good works, they must do what pleases father and mother or those who have authority over them in their parents' stead. Every child that knows this commandment and follows it, to begin with has the great inner comfort of being able, in the face of all who are involved with their own self-chosen works, to say with a sense of joy and satisfaction, "See, this work of mine pleases my God in heaven very much; that I know for sure." Let the rest, the entire crowd, come forward to boast of their many great, painful, and difficult works, and let us see if they can come up with a single one that is greater and nobler than obedience to father and mother, which God has commanded and thereby set next in rank to obedience to his own majesty. Where the Word and will of God are in use and are being observed, there nothing should count for more than the word and will of our parents, provided that these, too, remain subordinated to obedience toward God and do not run counter to the earlier commandments.

For this reason you should heartily rejoice and thank God that He has chosen and equipped you to do for Him such a precious and pleasing work. Even though many consider it most trifling and contemptible, make certain that you regard it as great and precious, not because of your worthiness, but because it is set within that jewel, within that holy shrine, the Word and commandment of God. O what a price wouldn't the Carthusian order, the monks and the nuns, pay if by means of all their religious exercises they could bring before God a single work performed in response to His command and if they could stand with a happy heart before Him and say, "Now I know that this work really pleases Thee." Where will these poor, miserable people be able to hide when in the presence of God and all the world their faces turn red with shame when they are confronted by some child that has lived up to this commandment and have to confess that despite their whole lifetime of effort they are not worthy to offer that child a drink of water? Serves them right for letting themselves be tricked by the devil's deceits and for trampling God's commandment under foot, so that they must now torture themselves with works of their own contrivance, only to be rewarded with ridicule and the loss of all their labor.

Should not your heart jump for joy and overflow with happiness that when it has gone to work and done what was commanded, it can say, "See, this is better than all the holiness of the Carthusians, even if they were to fast themselves to death or pray on their knees without ever getting up," Here you have a sure text and a divine testimony that this was God's command; but regarding their self-devised works He commanded not a word. Such, however, is the world's wretchedness and miserable blindness that nobody will believe this—so utterly has the devil bewitched us with sham holiness and the glitter of self-chosen works.

Therefore, I repeat, I really wish people would open their eyes and ears and take this to heart, so that we may not eventually be again deflected from God's pure Word to the devil's lying rubbish. All would then be well; parents would have more joy, love, kindness, and harmony in their homes, while children would completely win the love of their parents. On the other hand, if they are stubborn and will not do what they should unless a cane is laid to their shoulders, then they anger both God and their parents. Thereby they deprive themselves of their treasure, their joy of conscience, and reap nothing but trouble. This accounts for the things going on in the world that everybody is complaining about. Both young and old are quite out of hand and unmanageable; they have no sense of respect or honor; they will do nothing unless driven to it by force; they slander and put down one another behind each other's backs as much as they can. God therefore punishes so that they get into all sorts of trouble and misery. Usually the parents can do nothing about this, for it was simply a case of one fool raising another, and as the parents had lived, so live their children after them.

This, I say, should be the first great reason urging us to keep this commandment. If we had neither father nor mother, we ought on account of this commandment wish that God would set blocks of wood or stone before us that we might call our father and mother. How much more, when He has given us living parents, should we be glad to show them honor and obedience? For we know that this pleases the divine Majesty and all angels, irritates all the devils, and, in addition, is the greatest work that one can do next to the noble service of God set forth in the previous commandments. Not even gifts of charity nor any other service rendered to the neighbor can equal this work. For God has given the highest ranking to parenthood, making it, in fact, His representative on earth. That this is God's will and pleasure should be reason and motivation enough willingly and cheerfully to do whatever we can for our parents.

Moreover, it is our duty to show also before the world that we are grateful for the kindness and all the benefits received from our parents. But here again the devil rules in the world, with the result that children forget their parents, as all of us forget God and fail to consider how God feeds, guards, and shields us and how many good things He provides for our physical and spiritual welfare. Especially when an evil hour comes upon us, we angrily mutter our impatience and totally forget about all the good things we received throughout our life. We treat our parents the same way; yet there is not a child that recognizes and considers this, unless the Holy Spirit leads him to do so. God knows all about this perversity of the people of the world. This is why He keeps after them with the reminders and proddings of the commandments, so that everyone might think what his parents did for him. He who does think of this will find that he received his body and life from his parents, and also that he was fed and reared by them, without which care he would have choked a hundred times over in his own filth. Therefore it has been well and truly said by wise old people, *"Deo, parentibus, et magistris non potest satis gratiae rependi,"* that is, "One can never adequately thank and repay God, one's parents, and one's teachers." Anyone who recognizes this and thinks carefully about it will surely of his own accord show his parents every honor and esteem them highly as the ones through whom God bestowed everything good upon him.

Besides all this, there is another important reason to spur

us all the more to keep this commandment, namely, that God has attached a lovely promise to it by saying, "So that you may have long life in the land in which you dwell." There you see for yourself how tremendously serious God is about this commandment. For He not merely declares how much our obedience to this commandment pleases Him and what joy and delight it gives Him, but also that it will promote our success and welfare and enable us to lead a contented, pleasant life in the enjoyment of all kinds of good things. Therefore also St. Paul strongly emphasizes and highly praises this commandment in Ephesians 6:2-3: "This is the first commandment with a promise, 'that it may be well with you and that you may live long on the earth.'" Although promises are also implied in the other commandments, yet in none of them is the promise as clearly and expressly stated as here.

So then, there you have this commandment's fruit and reward: He who keeps it will have good days, happiness, and prosperity. On the other hand, for him who is disobedient, the penalty is that he will perish all the sooner without having had real joy in life. For in Scripture "to have long life" does not merely mean to live many years but to have everything that should go with long life, such as health, wife and offspring, peace, good government, etc., without which this life can neither be happily enjoyed nor continue for long. So if you do not want to obey father and mother nor let yourself be properly brought up by them, then go ahead and obey the hangman, and if not the hangman then the reaper Death. God, in short, insists that you obey Him, love Him, and serve Him, in which case He will richly reward you with every kind of good thing; but if you anger Him, He will send both death and the hangman after you.

Where do you suppose all the many rascals come from who daily must be hanged, beheaded, and executed, if not from their own disobedience? For they do not let themselves be trained with kindness. The result is that they bring themselves under God's punishment and into manifest misfortune and misery, for it rarely happens that such scoundrels die a normal death at a normal time of life.

The godly and the obedient, however, have God's blessing. They live long in the peaceful enjoyment of life. They see their children's children to "the third and fourth generation," as said above. Experience also shows that where there are fine, old families that flourish and have many children, it is obviously because some were well brought up and thought much of their parents. On the other hand, Psalm 109:13 says of a godless person: "May his posterity be cut off; may his name be blotted out in the second generation." So take to heart how important God considers obedience, since He values it so highly, is so greatly pleased with it, and rewards it so richly, and also punishes so strictly those who are disobedient.

All this I say in order that it might be impressed deeply on the young. For nobody believes how necessary, despite the fact that under the papacy it was not heeded nor taught, this commandment is. Everyone thinks these are such plain and simple words, words that in any case he knows well. So he skims over them lightly and begins gawking at something else, failing to see and realize how greatly he angers God when he bypasses this commandment and how precious and God-pleasing a work it is to keep it.

It belongs to the discussion of this commandment to say something also about the various kinds of obedience toward those superiors whose function it is to command and govern us. From the authority of parents all other kinds of authority flow out at various angles. When a father is not able to rear his child by himself, he draws in a schoolmaster to do the teaching; if the schoolmaster cannot do it, the father relies on the help of friends or neighbors; if the father is dying, he wills and delegates his authority and responsibility to others who are designated for that purpose. If he is to manage his household, then his servants, hired men, and maids must similarly be under his authority. Thus all who are called masters stand in the parents' stead, and it is from the parents that they must derive their power and authority to rule. This is why in Biblical usage they are called fathers, since their responsibility places them in the role of fathers who are to have a fatherly attitude toward those under them. So also from ancient times the Roman and other languages termed the master and the lady of the house *patres et matres familias*, that is, housefathers and housemothers. So also the Romans called their governors and rulers *patres patriae*, that is, fathers of the country. This puts us greatly to shame; we want to be Christians and yet do not refer to our rulers in such terms, or at least do not treat and honor them as fathers.

Now, what a child owes his father and mother, all members of the household likewise owe to them. Therefore, manservants and maids should see to it that they not only obey their masters and mistresses but also honor and esteem them as their own fathers and mothers, doing everything they know is expected of them, not reluctantly because they must, but gladly and with joy precisely for the reason just mentioned, that it is God's command and pleases Him more than all other works. So they ought even to be willing to pay for the opportunity of serving and should be glad when they acquire masters or mistresses, so that they can have the happy conscience that knows how to do the genuinely golden works. In the past these works were despised as insignificant, and everyone in the devil's name rushed into monasteries, on pilgrimages, and after indulgences, thus hurting themselves and their consciences.

If these things could be impressed upon people, then a servant girl would skip for joy as she goes about her work, praising and thanking God. The careful, tidy work by which she acquires food and pay would win her a treasure such as those who pass for the greatest saints do not have. Is it not a splendid thing when people are able to tell themselves, "If I do my daily housework well, that is better than the holiness and austere life of all the monks"? And besides this you have the assurance that everything will turn out great for you and that you will prosper. How could you live a more happy and holy life, as far as works are concerned? It is really faith that makes a person holy in the sight of God; faith serves God alone, while works serve the neighbor. So by faith you have every blessing, the Lord's sheltering protection, and, in addition, a carefree conscience and a gracious God who intends to reward you a hundredfold. This really makes you a nobleman—provided only that you are pious and obedient. If you are not that, then for a start you get nothing but the wrath and displeasure of God, a heart empty of peace, and finally all kinds of distresses and misfortunes.

Anyone whom this does not motivate toward godliness we shall hand over to the hangman and to Death the Reaper. Let everyone who can accept instruction therefore realize that God is not joking. He is speaking to you; he is demanding obedience of you. If you obey Him, then you are His dear child; if you despise His commandment, then take disgrace, misery, and anguish as your reward.

The same is to be said concerning obedience toward earthly authority, which, as has been stated, all comes under the heading of the parental office and radiates outward from it in all directions. The head of a country is a father not simply once but as many times over as there are inhabitants, citizens, or subjects under him. God provides for us and sustains us through our rulers, as through our parents, with food, house and home, protection, and security. And because civil authorities bear the name and title of "parent" as their highest medal of honor, we on our part owe them the honor of thinking highly of them as earth's greatest treasure and most precious jewel.

He who is obedient, willing, quick to be of service, and glad to give honor to whom it is due knows that God is pleased with him and that he will have joy and happiness as his reward. On the other hand, if he does not want to do these things out of love, but despises authority and rebels against it, let him know that he will receive none of God's grace and blessing. Where he expects his attitude to bring in one gold piece, he will elsewhere lose ten times as many. Or he will go to the gallows, or perish through war, pestilence, or famine, or his children will be a disappointment to him; he will find himself suffering injury, injustice, and violence at the hands of employees, neighbors, strangers, and tyrants. Thus we get paid and rewarded with what we set out for and deserve.

If we only would believe that deeds done in obedience to this commandment really do please God and are richly rewarded, then our lives would be simply flooded with blessings and we would have what our heart desires. But God's Word and commandment are held in contempt, as if they had come from some street vendor. Well, let us see if you are the man to defy God. Do you imagine that it will be hard for Him to pay you back? Your life would be so much more agreeable under God's kindness, peace, and blessing than under His disfavor and consequent misfortune. Why is the world, do you suppose, now so full of disloyalty, disgrace, misery, and murder? Is it not that everyone wants to be his own master, accountable to no superior, caring about no one, and doing only what pleases himself? So consequently God punishes one scoundrel by means of another. Thus when you cheat or despise your master, someone comes along to do the same to you, even to the point where what you have done will be paid back to you tenfold through what you will have to suffer at the hands of your own wife, children, or workers.

We all feel our misfortunes, of course, and we grumble about disloyalties, power plays, and injustices, but we refuse to see that we ourselves are rascals who thoroughly deserve such punishment and yet are not in the least improved by it.

We turn our backs on God's grace and blessing; therefore it is only right that we have nothing but misfortune, without any mercy whatever. Still, there must be some good people left on earth since God nevertheless still allows us so many blessings! But on the basis of what we ourselves deserve, we ought to be allowed not one penny in the house, not one spear of straw on the field. All of this I have had to teach with these many words in order that someone possibly might take them to heart for a change and we might get rid of the blindness and misery in which we are sunk so deeply and instead rightly perceive the Word and will of God and sincerely accept it. That Word could teach us how to obtain all the joy, prosperity, and salvation we need for time and eternity.

Thus far we have dealt with three classes of fathers included in this commandment: fathers by blood, fathers of households, and fathers of a nation. Besides these there are also the spiritual fathers, but I do not mean like those in the papacy. They did indeed let themselves be called fathers, but they performed no fatherly role. Only those are properly called spiritual fathers who govern and lead us by means of God's Word, as St. Paul boasts of himself as being a father, in 1 Corinthians 4:15, where he says: "I have begotten you in Christ Jesus through the Gospel." Since these are spiritual fathers, they are entitled to corresponding honor, even more than all other kinds of fathers. But in fact they are shown the least honor of all. The world's way of honoring them is to drive them out of the country and to begrudge them even a piece of bread. In short, they must be, as St. Paul says in 1 Corinthians 4:13, "the refuse of the world, the offscouring of all things."

Yet there is need to impress upon the people that those who want to be known as Christians owe it to God to regard those that watch over their souls as "worthy of double honor" (1 Timothy 5:17), to treat them well, and to provide for their well-being. God will in turn adequately provide for those who do this and will not let them suffer want. But here everyone resists and pulls back; all are afraid that their bellies will go hungry, and so they cannot bring themselves to support as much as a single faithful preacher, though formerly they kept 10 sleek paunches filled. For this we deserve that God should take His Word and His blessings away from us and once again let lying preachers arise who send us to the devil—besides squeezing us for our sweat and blood.

Those, however, who keep their eyes on God's will and

commandment have His promise to reward them richly for contributing to the support of their temporal or spiritual fathers and for honoring them. He promises not just that they shall have bread, clothing, and money for a year or two, but long life, the food to sustain it, and the peace to enjoy it, with eternal riches and blessedness to follow. So only do your duty, and leave it to God how He will support you and provide whatever you need. If He who has promised this has never yet lied to anyone, He will not lie to you either.

This ought always to encourage us and so touch our hearts and set them flowing with joy and love toward those to whom we owe honor that we lift our hands in joyful thanksgiving to the God who has given us such promises. To obtain their fulfillment we ought to be willing to run to the ends of the earth. For even if the whole world were to combine its efforts, it could not add one short hour to our life or raise one grain of wheat for us out of the soil. But God can and will give you everything in abundance according to the desires of your heart. Whoever despises this and tosses it to the winds is simply not worthy to hear any word from God.

More than enough has now been said to those to whom this commandment is directed.

It would be well in addition to address the parents in order to explain to them their office and how they should treat those committed to their authority. Although the Ten Commandments do not expressly state the duties of superiors, they are abundantly prescribed in many other passages of Scripture. God does wish them to be included specifically also in this commandment in which He speaks of father and mother. For God does not want scoundrels or tyrants to have this office and authority; nor does He grant this honor—the power and authority to govern—to certain persons in order that they may be objects of veneration. Rather, parents should recognize their responsibility to obey God and, above all, to be genuinely and faithfully concerned to fulfill all the duties of their office. These duties are fulfilled not only by providing for the material support of their children, servants, subjects, etc. but especially by training them to the praise and honor of God. So do not imagine that the parental office exists for your own pleasure and caprice. On the contrary, it is a matter of God's strict command and directive, and He it is who will hold you accountable for it.

Here again the trouble is that nobody observes and pays attention to these things. Everybody acts as if God gave us children for our pleasure and pastime, servants merely for us to work like oxen or horses, and subjects for us to treat as we please, as if we need not concern ourselves about what they learn or how they live. No one is willing to see that the divine Majesty has commanded our concern for them, that He will hold us strictly accountable for it, and that He will punish its neglect. Nor is it recognized how extremely important it is that we show a genuine interest in the young. If we want able and qualified persons as civil and spiritual leaders, then we really must spare no toil, trouble, or cost in teaching and educating our children to serve God and humanity. We must not think only of how to accumulate money and property for them. God is well able to provide for them and to make them rich, as He keeps doing every day. The reason He has given children into our charge is that we might train and govern them according to His will, as He has commanded us to do; otherwise God would have had no need of father or mother. Therefore let everyone know that he is required, as a matter of the highest duty and on pain of losing the favor of God, to bring up his children in reverent fear and knowledge of God, and if they are talented also to let them become educated so that their services can eventually be used where needed.

If we would do this, God would richly bless us and give us the grace to train persons to be the sort who would enrich the nation and the people. We would have good, capable citizens and virtuous, home-loving wives, who in turn would bring up their children and households to reverence God. Think about it yourself—what terrible harm you do if you neglect this and fail to bring up your child to be a useful and God-fearing person. You will bring guilt and wrath on yourself and thus earn hell by the way you treated your children, even if in other respects you were devout and without fault. It is because people ignore this commandment that God is punishing the world so terribly; discipline, good order, and peace have broken down, and we all complain about it but fail to see that it is our own fault. Our citizens are lawless and disobedient because of the way we train them.

Let this warning suffice. A fuller treatment of the matter will have to wait until a later time.

### The Fifth Commandment

*"Thou shalt not kill."*

Thus far we have considered both the spiritual and civil government, that is, both the divine and the paternal authorities, and the obedience due to each. In this next commandment we shall step outside of our own home and go out among our neighbors to learn how we and they should live together, how each one individually should conduct himself toward his fellow man. For this reason neither God nor the government are included in this commandment. Nor are they deprived in this commandment of their right to take human life. For God has delegated His authority to punish evildoers to the civil government acting in place of parents, who, as we read in Moses, formerly had to bring their children to judgment themselves and sentence them to death. Therefore what is forbidden here applies not to governments but to private individuals.

This commandment is simple enough. It is often discussed because one hears it at church once every year in the Gospel lesson from Matthew 5, where Christ Himself explains and summarizes it to the effect that we are forbidden to kill with our hands, in our hearts, by word, sign, or gesture, or by giving aid or offering counsel to a killer. The commandment forbids anger to everyone except, as stated earlier, to those who are the representatives of God, that is, parents and rulers. To be angry, to reprove, and to punish are prerogatives of God and His representatives, prerogatives that they are to exercise against those who transgress this and the other commandments.

The reason and necessity for this commandment is that, as God well knows, this world is wicked and this life full of trouble. Therefore He has set up this and the other commandments as a boundary wall between good and evil. Assaults of every sort are made against every commandment, and also against this one. Many of the people among whom we must live do us harm, so that we are given cause for being at enmity with them. For example, when your neighbor sees that you have received from God a better house and property or more riches and good fortune than he, he becomes irritated and envious and has nothing good to say about you.

Thus you acquire many enemies through the prompting of the devil. They begrudge you even the slightest physical or spiritual good. When we notice this attitude in them, our hearts want to retaliate with rage, bloodshed, and revenge. There follow curses and blows, and finally catastrophe and murder. Here God steps in and intervenes in kindly fashion like a father in order to settle the strife, so that misfortune is prevented and nobody gets hurt. In short, He intends to protect and deliver everyone and give him security against the outrage and violence of others. To that end He has set up this commandment as a citadel, stronghold, and shelter around a neighbor so that no one may do him bodily hurt or harm.

It is therefore the sense of this commandment that one should do no one an injury on account of some wrong he has done, even though he very much deserves it. For if murder is forbidden, so is everything that may lead up to it. Many a person, though he does not actually commit bloodshed, nevertheless calls down curses on someone in the hope that they might soon put an end to him on whom they fall. Desire for revenge clings to our nature, and it is commonly accepted that no one will stand for being injured by anyone else. Therefore God wants to do away with the root and source of bitterness toward our neighbor. He wants us to develop the habit of keeping this commandment before our eyes at all times, of seeing ourselves mirrored in it, and of respecting God's will, so that we may confidently and prayerfully commit to Him any wrongs we have suffered. Then we shall let our foes rant and rage and do their worst. Thus we may learn to calm our anger and acquire a patient, gentle heart, especially toward those who give us cause to be angry, namely our enemies.

The whole sum and substance of the commandment against killing, as it is to be clearly and distinctly impressed upon people in general, is this: In the first place, we are not to harm any one. This means, to begin with, that we are not to hurt him by means of some physical act. Next, we are not to use our tongue for suggesting or advising that physical injury should be done to someone. Also, we should neither use nor sanction any means or methods by which anyone might be harmed. And finally, our heart should not be hostile to anyone nor wish him ill in a spirit of anger and hatred. Thus you should keep your body and soul blameless over against all people, especially over against those who wish you ill or who do you harm. As for doing evil against someone who wishes you well and does what is for your good, that is not even human; it is devilish.

In the second place, not only is that person guilty of violating this commandment who does the evil that it forbids, but also the one who fails to take the opportunity to do good to his neighbor and who, though able to prevent evil and to protect, shield, and save the neighbor from injury and bodily harm, fails to do so. If, then, you send a person away naked when you might have given him clothing, you have let him freeze to death. If you see someone hungry and do not feed him, then you have let him starve to death. Likewise, if you see someone condemned to die or in similar peril and fail to rescue him although you know ways and means of doing so, then you have killed him. Your plea that you contributed no word or deed to the killing will not do you any good. For you did withhold your love from him and robbed him of the help that might have saved his life.

Therefore God rightly calls all those persons murderers who fail to give counsel and aid to those who are in need and in peril of body and life. God will pass a most terrible sentence upon them on judgment day, as Christ himself declares. He will say: "I was hungry and you gave Me no food, I was thirsty and you gave Me no drink, I was a stranger and you did not welcome Me, naked and you did not clothe Me, sick and in prison and you did not visit Me" (Matthew 25:42-43). That is to say, "You were willing to let Me and My followers die of hunger, thirst, and cold, be torn to pieces by wild beasts, rot in prison, and perish in dire distresses."

What is this but His rebuke directed against murderers and bloodhounds? For although you did not physically perform these criminal acts, nevertheless, as far as you were concerned, you let your neighbor remain stuck in his misfortune until he perished. This is the same as if I were to see someone struggling in deep water or fallen into a fire and yet would not reach out my hand to him to pull him out and save him. Would not all the world recognize me as nothing but a scoundrel and a murderer?

Therefore God's real meaning in this commandment is that we should allow no one to come to any harm, but should show kindness and love to everyone, especially, as I said, to those who are our enemies. For to show kindness to one's friends is no more than a common heathen virtue, as Christ declares in Matthew 5:46-47.

Here, then, we again have God's Word by which He intends to stir us up and spur us on to true, noble, and exalted conduct such as gentleness and patience and, in short, love and kindness toward our enemies. He wishes to keep reminding us always to recall the First Commandment, about His being our God, that is, the One who wants to help us, to stand by us, and to protect us, so that He may suppress in us the desire for revenge.

43

If this were persistently and thoroughly impressed on people, then we would have our hands full doing good works. But this preaching would not do for monks! It would detract too much from the "spiritual estate," get too much under the skin of the Carthusians and their holiness, practically forbid their kind of good works, and empty the monasteries. For this teaching would rate the ordinary Christian life as being just as worthy as theirs, indeed far more worthy. Everybody would be able to see how the monks trick and mislead the world with a false, hypocritical show of sanctity. For they have thrown this and the other commandments to the winds, having taken them to be unnecessary, as if they were not commands but mere counsels. In addition, they have shamelessly paraded and loudly trumpeted their hypocritical ways and works as "the most perfect life." This they did in order to have a cushy, easy life without crosses and without any need for patience under suffering. This is why they ran into monasteries, so that they would not need to suffer wrongs from anyone nor do good to anyone. You, however, are to realize that the true, holy, divine works are those which God's Word commands. Over such works God and all His angels rejoice. The reverse is true of all the saintliness devised by men; it is but stench and filth, deserving nothing but wrath and damnation.

## The Sixth Commandment

*"Thou shalt not commit adultery."*

In light of the previous commandment, those that follow are easy to understand. They all proceed from the central point that one should guard against doing any sort of harm to the neighbor. They are arranged in excellent sequence. First there is the focus on the person of our neighbor. Next in the sequence comes the focus on the person closest to him, the one who is his dearest treasure next to his own life, namely his wife, who is one flesh and blood with him. There is no possession of his through which greater injury could be done to him. Therefore, this commandment explicitly forbids dishonoring his wife. The emphasis here is particularly upon adultery, because marriage was obligatory among the Jewish people. Young people were married as early as possible. The state of virginity had no special status among them, neither was public prostitution and whoring tolerated as they are today. Thus adultery was the most common form of unchastity among them.

Since among us there is such a disgraceful mess and sludge of all manner of vice and lewdness, this commandment is aimed against every form of unchastity, whatever its name. Not only is the external act prohibited, but also every kind of source, stimulation, and means. Your heart, the words of your mouth, and your whole body are to be chaste. They are to allow no room, give no assistance, and offer no encouragement to unchastity. And that is not all. You are to defend, protect, and rescue your neighbor whenever he is in need or danger in respect to these matters. On the positive side, you are to help and guide your neighbor so that he may keep his honor. For if you are able to prevent a wrong and yet fail to do so, or if you close your eyes to it as if it were no concern of yours, then you are just as guilty as the evildoer himself. In short, everyone is required both to live a clean life himself and to help his neighbor to do the same. Thus, by means of this commandment God wants every husband and every wife to be guarded and protected against any trespassing.

This commandment is focused specifically on marriage and thus gives us occasion to speak of this estate. Let us therefore first of all note carefully how very highly God honors and extols married life by giving it His sanction and protection in the Ten Commandments. He sanctioned it earlier in the Fourth Commandment, "You shall honor your father and your mother." But here, as I said, he safeguards and protects it. Therefore he wants to see it honored, upheld, and treated also by us as being divinely instituted and full of blessing. For He established it as the first one of all His institutions, and He created man and woman with obvious differences, not for wickedness, but that they may be and remain attracted to each other, be fruitful, have children, care for them, and bring them up to the glory of God.

God has therefore most richly blessed marriage above all other estates. In addition, everything that the world contains He has assigned and devoted to providing marriage amply and richly with all that it needs. Married life is not a matter for jesting or impertinence; it is something splendid, the object of serious divine care and concern. That persons be brought up to serve the world and to promote knowledge of God, godly life, and virtue of every kind, and to fight wickedness and the devil—these are matters that have the highest priority with God.

Therefore I have always taught that we should not look down upon marriage or undervalue it as the blind world and the false clergy are doing. We are rather to view it in the light of the Word of God, which adorns and sanctifies it. Marriage is not merely to be placed on a level with other estates; it is to be put ahead and above them all, whether that be emperor, princes, bishops, or anyone else. Whatever status the spiritual and civil estates may have, they must nevertheless humble themselves and, as we shall hear, permit anyone to enter the estate of matrimony. Marriage is therefore not an exceptional state, but the most universal and noblest one, extending throughout Christendom and even the entire world.

Remember, in the second place, that marriage is not only an honorable but also a necessary estate, one that is solemnly commanded by God. In general, men and women of every circumstance, having been created for it, belong in marriage. Yet there are some (though few) exceptions, whom God has specially exempted—those who are not equipped for married life and others whom by means of a high supernatural gift He has released from it, enabling them to maintain chastity outside of marriage. Where nature as implanted by God has its way, it is not possible to remain chaste except within marriage. For flesh and blood remain flesh and blood, and the natural tendencies and attractions proceed without restraint or hindrance, as everyone can see and sense. Therefore, in order that it might be easier to avoid unchastity in some measure, God has established marriage so that everyone may have his assigned portion and be happy with it, although even here the grace of God is needed to keep the heart pure.

From this you see how the papal crowd of priests, monks, and nuns resist God's order and commandment when they disdain and forbid marriage and presume to vow that they will maintain eternal chastity, besides deceiving the general public with lying words and false appearances. For no one has such little love and desire for chastity as precisely those who under cover of great sanctity avoid marriage and either indulge openly and shamelessly in fornication or secretly carry on in even worse fashion, in ways one does not dare mention, as has all too often come to light. In short, even if they avoid the act, yet their hearts are so full of unchaste thoughts and evil desires that they burn with perpetual secret passion. All this can be circumvented in married life. Therefore this commandment condemns and cancels all vows of chastity outside of marriage; yes, it even commands all poor, captive consciences deceived by their monastic vows to leave their unchaste existence and enter married life. It does this in view of the fact that, even if their monastic life were godly in other respects, yet the maintenance of chastity is beyond its power, and if they remain in monastic life, they will inevitably only sin all the more and all the longer against this commandment.

I am saying this in order that young people may be urged to acquire a love for married life and know that it is a blessed estate pleasing to God. Thus in time one might again turn the situation around to the point where marriage would again be honored and there would be a reduction of wild, disorderly conduct such as is now everywhere prevalent in public prostitution and other disgraceful vices resulting from contempt for married life. Parents and civil authorities therefore have the duty of supervising the young so that they are brought up to live disciplined and respectable lives, and when they are grown, become honorably married in the fear of God. God will then add his blessing and grace so that people find joy and happiness in marriage.

In conclusion, let it be said that this commandment requires that everyone not only should live his life, particularly also his married life, in chastity of thought, word, and deed but also should love and treasure the wife or husband given by God. For maintaining marital chastity, husband and wife must above all things live together in love and harmony, each loving the other with the whole heart and with totally committed faithfulness. This is one of the primary factors in the creation of a love and a desire for chastity. Where such loving harmony prevails, chastity can be expected to follow of itself without any commands. This is why St. Paul so diligently admonishes husbands and wives to love and honor each other. So here you have another precious good work—in fact, many and great good works—that you can joyfully set above all "spiritual estates" that are chosen without God's Word and commandment.

### The Seventh Commandment

#### "Thou shalt not steal."

The thing dearest to a person next to his own self and his spouse is his temporal property. This, too, God wants to have protected. He has forbidden us to get our neighbor's property away from him or to diminish it. For stealing is nothing other than acquiring someone else's property by unjust means.

Briefly stated, this includes taking advantage of our neighbor to his loss in any sort of dealing. Now, stealing is a widespread, common vice, but so little notice is taken of it that it has gotten very much out of hand. If all who are thieves but do not want to admit it were strung up on the gallows, the world would soon be emptied and there would not be enough gallows and hangmen. For, as I just stated, it is not only when a man's strongbox or his pocket are cleaned out that it is to labeled theft, but also when someone takes advantage of his neighbor in the marketplace, grocery store, butcher shop, wine or beer cellar, or workshop, in short, wherever people do business and exchange money for goods or services.

Let us draw the picture in somewhat sharper outline for the common people, so that we can at least see how honest we really are. Suppose, for example, that a manservant or maid is not faithful in service, causes damage to property, or allows damage to be done although able to prevent it. Or suppose that a worker in some other way neglects or wastes property through laziness, carelessness, or spite intended to vex and annoy the employer. When this is done intentionally (for I am not speaking of what is accidental or unintentional), a worker could cheat the employer out of 30 or 40 gold pieces a year. If someone had taken such sums by theft he would be strangled with a noose, but here you dare to be defiant and insolent and challenge anyone to call you a thief.

The same can be said of those mechanics, workmen, and day laborers who act high-handedly, seemingly unable to figure out enough ways to overcharge people, and who yet are careless and unreliable in their work. These are all much worse than sneak thieves, against whom one can at least install locks and bolts or can deal with them, when they are caught, in such a manner that they do not steal again. But no one can guard himself against those others. No one as much as dares to give them a hard look or accuse them of a single theft. One would ten times rather lose money out of the wallet. For these persons are my neighbors, my good friends, my own servants, from each one of whom I expect good treatment, and yet they are the very first to defraud me.

Similarly, dishonest practices are in full force also in markets and in ordinary business places. There people openly cheat each other with defective merchandise, dishonest measure, false weights, and bad coins, and one person takes advantage of another by means of trickery, sharp practices, and underhanded dealings. Or again, one person swindles another in trade and deliberately exploits, fleeces, and victimizes him. Who can tell or imagine all that goes on? Thievery is, in short, the most common craft and the largest trade union on earth. When humankind is analyzed at all its levels, it turns out to be simply one great, wide warehouse full of superthieves. Therefore these men are called swivel chair swindlers, land-grabbers and highway robbers. Far from being cookie-jar or cash-box sneak thieves, they sit in office chairs and pass for good fellows and honorable, decent citizens, and yet under cover of a fine show of legality they engage in robbery and theft.

Yes, here one might well keep quiet about individual petty thieves if one could only get at the great, powerful superthieves who associate with the influential and the great and who daily plunder not merely a city or two but the entire country. Ah, what would then become of their chief, the high protector of all thieves, the holy see at Rome, together with all its following, which by thievery has taken over the treasures of the world and holds them to this day?

In short, the way of the world is this: Those who can openly steal and rob go about freely, safe from reprimand by anyone, and even expect to be honored. Meanwhile, the little sneak thieves whose hands on occasion have dipped into a till must bear the disgrace and penalty of it in order that by comparison the others will look decent and respectable. But those others should know that before God they are the greatest thieves of all, and that He will punish them exactly as they deserve.

Since, as we have shown, the range of this commandment extends so far, it is necessary to hold it up before the crowd and to keep underscoring it. They should not be allowed simply to go on without restraint; instead, the wrath of God should always be kept before their eyes and urgently impressed upon them. For this is something we must preach not so much to Christians, but chiefly to rascals and scoundrels. The judge, the jailor, and the hangman should really be preaching at them. Let everyone know, then, that he is duty bound, at the risk of God's displeasure, to do no harm to his neighbor, to take no advantage of him in business, and never in any kind of transaction to deal unreliably or underhandedly with him. More than that, he is faithfully to protect his neighbor's property and to look after and further his interests, especially if he is paid or otherwise remunerated for such services.

A person who willfully ignores this commandment may indeed get by with it and evade the hangman, but God's wrath and punishment he will not escape. Though he may long carry on in his insolent, arrogant course, yet he will remain the tramp and bum that he is, and to top it off he will suffer all kinds of trouble and misfortune. You who ought to be taking care of your employers' property, which enables you to fare sumptuously, blithely accept wages for your thievery and in addition expect to be treated as very important persons. There are many of you who are even insolent toward your employers and unwilling to do them the favor and service of protecting them from losses. But listen to what you will get for it. When you have acquired property of your own and have your own household—which God will help you get for your undoing—the tables will be turned and you will be paid in kind for what you have done. Every penny you pilfered and every penny's worth of damage you caused, you will have to pay for thirty times over.

It will be the same for workmen and laborers who nowadays subject us to their intolerable gall. They impose on us, acting as if they were lords over the property of others with a right to all that they demand. Well, let them brazenly rip off people as long as they can. God will not forget His commandment. He will pay them according to their deserts and hang them not on a green tree but on the even more dishonorable dry tree of the gallows. As long as they live they will neither prosper nor succeed. Of course, if our government were properly in control, it would soon be possible to clamp down on their insolence. The ancient Romans, for example, would immediately get at such fellows and let them have it, so that others had to take warning.

The same sort of thing will happen to those who turn the open public market into a wrecker's yard and robbers' den. They daily take advantage of the poor, imposing new burdens, raising the prices. Everyone misuses the market in whatever way he pleases, being arrogant and conceited about it as well, as if he had the right and privilege to sell at whatever exorbitant price he wishes without criticism from anyone. We shall stand aside to watch how they fleece, grab, and hoard. But we shall put our trust in God, who will in any case take matters into His own hands. After they have long scrimped and scraped, He will speak this kind of blessing upon their efforts: "The grain in your granary and the beer in your cellar will spoil, and the cattle in your barn will die. Yes, where you have cheated and defrauded anyone out of a single dollar, that dollar will eventually rust and eat away everything you have piled up, so that you will never enjoy it."

It is a matter of daily observation and experience that stolen property or ill-gotten gain never thrives. How many there are who scrape and scratch day and night and yet are not a cent richer for it! And though they gather a pile, they have to suffer so much trouble and misfortune that they cannot enjoy it or pass it on to their children. But because we are all apathetic and go along as if these things were no concern of ours, God must find another way to get at us to teach us morals. He sends us one tax increase after another, or He invites in a troop of toughs, who in one hour clean out safe and purse to the last penny and then, by way of thanks, burn and ravage house and home and outrage and kill wife and children.

In short, however much you steal, you can expect that again as much will surely be stolen from you; and whoever takes anything by force or gains it by dishonest means must put up with someone else of the same stripe who will beat him at his own game. Since everyone robs and steals from everyone else, God shows Himself master of the art of punishing one thief by means of another. If it were not for this, where would we find ropes and gallows enough for the job?

Now, whoever is willing to listen, let him know that here is the commandment of God and that it is not meant for a joke. Although you may despise, cheat, rob, and steal from us, we shall manage to endure and bear up under your arrogance; and in the spirit of the Lord's Prayer we shall forgive and show mercy. For the upright will continue to have enough, while you will be hurting yourself more than you hurt others. But beware when you are approached by one of the now so numerous poor who must live from hand to mouth. If you act as if everyone's life depends on your generosity, if you skin him and scrape him to the bare bones, and if you even turn him away with proud arrogance though you ought to have freely given him aid, he will go away sad and dejected, and because he has no one to whom he can complain, he will cry aloud to heaven. I say again, beware of this as of the devil himself. For that poor man's sighs and prayers will not be spoken in jest; they will have such an effect that you and all the world will find it too heavy to bear. Those sighs and prayers will press through and reach the One who has compassion on the poor and the distressed and will see to it that they are not unavenged. But if you disdain this and are defiant, then see whom you have brought upon your back. If ever you really succeed and prosper, you can denounce both God and me before the whole world as being liars.

We have now exhorted, warned, and admonished you enough. Anyone who refuses to pay attention to this and believe it, let him go his own way until experience teaches him his lesson. However, this needs to be impressed on young people, so that they may take care not to get involved with the old, disorderly crowd, but keep their eyes focused on God's commandment lest divine wrath and punishment overtake them, too. Our responsibility is simply to instruct and reprove by means of God's Word. As for restraining open lawlessness, that is the responsibility of rulers and magistrates. They are to notice what is going on, and they are to have the courage to establish and maintain order in every kind of business and trade in order that the poor may not be burdened and crushed and in order that they themselves may not become guilty of others men's sins.

Enough has been said to explain what stealing is. One should not define it too narrowly, but extend it to all our dealings with our neighbors. To sum up briefly, as in the case of the previous commandments: To begin with, we are here forbidden to harm or wrong our neighbor in any conceivable way, be it by inflicting loss or damage on his possessions and property or by withholding or interfering with their use; we are not even to approve or allow such wrongs, but are to check and prevent them. On the contrary, we are commanded to promote our neighbor's property interests, improve his situation, and if he is in need, be he friend or foe, share with him and lend to him.

Anyone who is looking for and really wants to do good works will here find an overabundance of things that please and delight the heart of God. Moreover, God lavishes wonderful blessings upon whatever is done in accordance with this commandment. We will be richly rewarded for every useful and friendly deed we do for our neighbor, as King Solomon teaches in Proverbs 19:17: "He who is kind to the poor lends to the Lord, and He will repay him for his deed." You have a rich Lord. Having Him, you surely have everything you need, and He will not let you suffer any lack or want. Thus you will be able with a happy conscience to enjoy a hundred times more than you could scrape together by irresponsible conduct and unjust dealings. Whoever does not care for this blessing will find wrath and misfortune aplenty.

### The Eighth Commandment

*"Thou shalt not bear false witness against thy neighbor."*

In addition to one's own person, one's wife or husband, and one's temporal possessions, there is a further treasure that the individual cannot do without, namely honor and good reputation. Living in human society is tolerable only if one is not in public disgrace or contempt. Therefore God does not want the neighbor's reputation, honor, and character, any more than his money and property, taken from him or diminished; he wants everyone to enjoy the respect of his wife, children, servants, and neighbors. As the words stand ("you shall not bear false witness"), the first and most obvious sense of this commandment relates to public courts of justice, where a poor, falsely accused man is subjected to abuse by false witnesses and as a result is penalized in body, possessions, or reputation.

In our time this kind of thing seems not to concern us much, but among the Jews it happened very often. That nation was organized under a fine, orderly government, and where there is such a government, there this sin will occur. The reason is that when judges, mayors, princes, or others in authority dispense justice, then it happens without fail in the world's normal course that there is a reluctance to offend anyone. So people instead use deceptive speech aimed at gaining favor, money, improved prospects, or friendship; and the result is that a man who is poor gets crushed, loses his case, and receives a penalty.

Everywhere in the world there is this prevailing misfortune that men of integrity seldom preside as judges in courts of law. Above everything else a judge ought to be an upright man, and not only an upright but also a wise, sensible, brave, and fearless man. By the same token, also a witness should be fearless; he should above all have integrity. For anyone who is to make right judgments and vigorous, clear-cut decisions is bound often to anger his good friends, relatives, neighbors, and some rich, powerful men who are in a position either to make or to break him. He must therefore in one respect be totally blind, keeping his eyes and ears closed to everything except the evidence placed before him, and he must let that evidence alone determine his decision.

This commandment, then, points first of all to the requirement that everyone should help his neighbor to his rights. He should not permit these to be violated or distorted. He should instead, whether as judge or as witness, uphold the next man's rights and stand guard over them, whatever their nature. This is to be the aim especially of our lawyers. They are to see to the justice and equity of every case. They should let right remain right, not distorting or beclouding or concealing any evidence out of consideration for money, property, status, or power. This particular aspect of the commandment, its reference to whatever happens in a courtroom, is its most obvious meaning.

Moreover, the commandment reaches a great deal farther if applied to spiritual jurisdiction and authority. Here, too, everyone bears false witness against his neighbor. For wherever there are godly preachers and Christians, the world considers them heretics, renegades, even inflammatory, desperate scoundrels. Besides this, God's Word itself is subjected to most shameful and venomous persecutions. It is slandered, contradicted, twisted out of shape, misinterpreted, and misapplied. It is always the way of the blind world to condemn and persecute the truth and the children of God without recognizing that this is sin.

Third, with regard to us all, this commandment forbids sins of language that may harm or offend our neighbor. Speaking false witness is obviously an action of the vocal tract. Thus God forbids all sins of the tongue against one's neighbor. This applies to false preachers with their deceptive teachings and blasphemies and to the false judges and witnesses with their perverse statements in court as well as their lying and malevolent talk outside of the courtroom. Included is especially the repulsive, shameful vice of scandalmongering or slander, by which the devil gets into our driver's seat. There is much one could say about this. Human nature is infected with this common disease, that one rather hears evil than good about one's neighbor. And though we ourselves are evil, we cannot stand to have anyone speak evil of us. Every one of us would like all the world to say nothing about him but words of golden goodwill; yet we cannot bear it when we hear the best spoken of others.

Therefore, in order to avoid such habitual sinning with the

tongue, we should note that no one has authority publicly to judge and reprove his neighbor, not even if he has seen him commit a sin, unless he has specifically been given the authority to judge and reprove. For there is indeed a great difference between these two: judging a sin and knowing about a sin. Knowing about a sin does not involve the right to sit in judgment on it. I am of course able to see and hear my neighbor sinning, but I have no business reporting it all around town. If I poke my nose in and judge and condemn, then I fall into a worse sin than his. So when you get to know about a sin, let your ear become its grave and shovel the dirt in on top of it and do not resurrect it until the day you are appointed judge and thus have the duty to administer punishment by virtue of your office.

Those are to be labeled scandalmongers who are not content with what they know but rush forward to pass sentence. When they have heard some tidbit, they carry it to every corner, relishing and delighting in rolling up someone else's dirt like pigs that wallow in the muck and root around in it with their snouts. By setting themselves up as judges, they are simply usurping God's judgment and office, pronouncing verdict and sentence in the most severe judgmental manner. For no judge can go further or reprove more sharply than to pronounce someone a thief, murderer, traitor, etc. Therefore, whoever presumes to say such things about his neighbor, invades the authority of the head of state and all magistrates. For although you do not wield the sword, yet you nevertheless ply your poisonous tongue to the disgrace and injury of your neighbor.

God therefore wants to check everyone from speaking evil of another, even when that person is known to be guilty. If the thing is not actually known, but was picked up only by hearsay, God all the more urgently forbids you to speak about it. But perhaps you say, "Why can't I talk about it if it is the truth?" My answer is, "Why don't you bring it before a proper judge?" "Oh, but I can't publicly prove it; it might be thrown back in my teeth and I be packed off in disgrace." Ah, friend, can't you smell the roast burning? If you do not trust yourself to come before the proper authorities to make your charges, then keep your mouth shut. What you do know for sure keep to yourself and do not share it with anyone. For by repeating the story you will seem a liar even if the story is true, since you cannot prove it. Besides, you would be acting like a scoundrel, because no one should deprive another of his honor and reputation unless these have already been taken away from him publicly.

Thus every report that cannot be substantiated in the proper public manner is false witness. Therefore, no one should make public or assert as true anything that is not already public on the basis of sufficient evidence. In short, what is secret should be allowed to remain secret, or at any rate should be reproved only in private, as we shall hear. When you meet someone with a loose tongue who gossips about others and slanders them, let him have it straight from your shoulder and make him blush for shame. In this way many a mouth can be stopped that would otherwise make some poor man so much the talk of the town that he can hardly clear his name. Honor and reputation can be destroyed in a moment, but cannot soon be restored.

As you can see, we are absolutely forbidden to say anything bad about our neighbor. There is an exception, however, in the case of civil authorities, preachers, and parents; for we must understand this commandment in such a way that evil is not allowed to go unpunished. We remember that according to the Fifth Commandment physical injury is to be inflicted by no one except the hangman. By virtue of his office, he does not do any good to his neighbor but only harm and evil. Yet the hangman does not sin against God's commandment, because God Himself instituted that office, having reserved to Himself the right to punish in whatever way He pleases as He warns us in [the appendix to] the First Commandment. Likewise, although no one has in his own person the right to judge or condemn another, yet if those whose duty it is to judge fail to do so, they are sinning as much as the person who does so on his own without having been given the authority. For in those cases necessity demands that one report the wrongdoing, prefer charges, present evidence, examine, and testify. The situation is the same as that of a doctor who, in treating a patient, must sometimes examine and handle the patient's genitals. Similarly, civil authorities, parents, even brothers and sisters and other good friends share the obligation to reprove evil when it is necessary and helpful to do so.

But the right way to go about this would be to follow the order given in the Gospel, in Matthew 18:15, where Christ says, "If your brother sins against you, go and tell him his fault, between you and him alone." Here you have a fine, most valuable lesson on how to rule the tongue, a lesson we should carefully note in order to avoid the repulsive sins of the tongue. Conduct yourself according to this rule so as not to begin talking behind your neighbor's back and spreading reports about him, but rather admonish him privately in order to help him to change. Likewise, if someone whispers in your ear what this or that person is supposed to have done, tell the whisperer to go himself and reprove the man in case he saw him doing the wrong, but if he did not see it, tell him to keep his mouth shut.

From the daily management of a household you can learn the same lesson. This is what the master of the house does when he sees a servant not doing his job: he speaks directly to the servant himself. If he would be so foolish as to leave his servant at home while he himself goes out on the streets to complain to the neighbors, he would probably be told, "Why, you fool! What concern is that of ours? Why don't you speak to the man himself?" That would really be a brotherly thing to do, for the evil would thus be corrected, and your neighbor would retain his honor. As Christ Himself says in the same Matthew 18 passage, "If he listens to you, you have gained your brother." Thereby you will have done a fine, splendid deed. Or do you imagine that it is something insignificant to gain a brother? Let all monks and holy orders with all their works piled together in one heap step forward, and let us see if they can come up with a single instance to their credit where they have won a brother!

Christ teaches further: "If he does not listen, take one or two others along with you, that every word may be confirmed by the evidence of two or three witnesses" (Matthew 18:16). So we are never to gossip behind anyone's back, but are always to deal personally with the individual concerned. If this fails, then bring the matter publicly before the people, either the civil or the ecclesiastical tribunal. There you will not stand alone, but will have with you those witnesses through whom you can convict the guilty person; on the basis of their testimony the judge can make his decision and issue the sentence. If this orderly, proper procedure is used, it is possible that the evildoer can be restrained or even reformed. But if you go around gossiping about someone in every corner and rooting around in the filth, nobody will be reformed; and afterwards when you are called up as a witness, you will try to deny having said anything. It will serve you right to have such gossipmongering spoiled for you and to have you set up as a warning to others. If your aim had been the improvement of your neighbor or love for the truth, you would not have been sneaking about secretly and shunning the open light of day.

Up to this point the reference has been to secret sins. But where the sin is so public that the judge and everyone else are aware of it, then you can without sinning avoid and abandon the wrongdoer as one who has brought the disgrace on himself, and you may also witness publicly against him. For when the thing is out in the open, there can be no question of slander or injustice or false witness. For example, we now censure the pope and his teachings, which are openly presented in books and shouted to all the world. For when the sin is public, it stands to reason that its punishment also should be public in order that everyone may know how to guard against it.

The sum and substance of this commandment, then, is this: No one shall harm his neighbor with his tongue, be he friend or foe. We are not to say anything bad about him whether the statement is true or false. The only exception is whatever must be said as a matter of official duty or for the purpose of helping the wrongdoer to change. We are to use the tongue only to speak the best we can about everyone, covering his sins and weaknesses by presenting them in the best light possible and by veiling them behind his more honorable and attractive qualities. The main reason for our doing this should be what Christ points out in the Gospel in a passage intended to embrace all of the commandments concerning our neighbor: "Whatever you wish that men would do to you, do so to them" (Matthew 7:12).

Nature teaches us the same thing by means of our own bodies. St. Paul says in 1 Corinthians 12:22-23: "The parts of the body that seem to be weaker are indispensable, and those parts of the body that we think less honorable we invest with the greater honor; and our unpresentable parts are treated with greater modesty." No one covers up his face, eyes, nose, and mouth; they need no covering, for they are the most honorable members that we have. But we do conceal carefully our weakest members, those of which we are ashamed. Our hands, eyes, and the rest of the body must help to cover and disguise them. So, in our relations with each other, we should screen whatever flaws or infirmities we notice in our neighbor, doing everything we can to serve, help, and promote his good standing in the community. On the other hand, we should ward off from him whatever tends to his disgrace. It is a particularly fine and noble virtue always to explain in the best possible terms and to put the best construction on whatever we hear about our neighbor—provided it is not a public scandal—and to defend him against the poisonous tongues of gossipmongers, who busy themselves wherever they can by digging out and raking together something to criticize in the neighbor, misconstruing things in the worst way and turning them wrong side out. This is now happening especially to the precious Word of God and to those who preach it.

This commandment, then, embraces a mighty great number of good works that are most highly pleasing to God and that bring with them an overflow of favors and blessings. If only these were recognized by the blind world and the false saints! For there is nothing about a man or in a man that can do greater and more far-reaching good in spiritual or in temporal matters than this smallest and weakest of his members, the tongue—or that can do greater or more far-reaching harm.

## The Ninth and Tenth Commandments

*"Thou shalt not covet thy neighbor's house."*

*"Thou shalt not covet thy neighbor's wife, nor his manservant, nor his maidservant, nor his cattle, nor anything that is thy neighbor's."*

These two commandments were, strictly speaking, given exclusively to the Jews. They nevertheless apply in part also to us. The Jews did not interpret them as being concerned with unchastity or theft, which sins were adequately forbidden in previous commandments. They imagined, however, that they were keeping them by outwardly obeying the commands and prohibitions contained in them. God therefore added these last two commandments so that they would realize that to covet a neighbor's wife or property or to have any designs whatever upon them is sinful and forbidden by God. These commandments were necessary especially because under Jewish rule manservants and maidservants did not have the freedom, as they do now, of serving for wages for as long a period as they wish. Instead, they themselves and all their possessions were the property of their master the same as his animals and the other things he owned. Every man also had the power publicly to dismiss his wife by giving her a letter of divorce in order to take a different wife. They had to recognize the possibility that if someone among them took a liking to another's wife, he might on some pretext put away his own wife and alienate the other man's wife from him in order to be able to take her legally for himself. They did not take this to be a sin or disgrace any more than for an employer nowadays to dismiss his own employees or to induce his neighbor's employees to leave their jobs.

I therefore say that although these commandments do have wider and higher application, the Jews correctly interpreted these commandments to mean that no one, not even under a specious pretext or a show of right, should desire or scheme to deprive the neighbor of what belongs to him, for example, his wife, servants, house and lot, fields, meadows, or cattle. The seventh commandment, above, forbids us to take from our neighbor or withhold from him his property to which we have no right. But here in these two commandments it is also forbidden to entice anything away from the neighbor, even though you would lose no honor in the eyes of the world by doing so and no one would accuse or dare to criticize you as having dealt fraudulently.

Such is human nature that no one wants another to have as much as he himself has. Everyone tries to get all he can and lets the next man look out for himself. Yet we all want to seem upright, we put up the best front we can, and we try to keep the scoundrel within us hidden. We think up subtle devices and under the guise of fairness use sly maneuvers (improved versions of which are devised every day). About this we dare to boast brazenly, insisting that it be called shrewdness and good business sense, not dishonesty. We are abetted in this by jurists and lawyers who bend and stretch the law to suit their case, straining and misapplying words with no regard for equity or the neighbor's needs. In short, he who is most adept and clever at such games gets the best advantage out of the law, and, as the saying goes, "The law favors the alert."

Thus this last commandment is not addressed to those whom the world considers scoundrels, but precisely to the most respectable—to those who look for approval as being decent and upright and who have not offended against the foregoing commandments. The Jews especially claimed to belong to this class, a claim made by many great nobles, lords, and princes also today. The ordinary masses belong farther down the scale under the Seventh Commandment; when they acquire possessions they do not much bother to ask whether they are observing right and honorable means.

The situation to which this commandment applies occurs most often in lawsuits by which someone attempts to get or squeeze something out of his neighbor. When people, for example, squabble and wrangle over a large inheritance, a piece of real estate, etc., they drag in and put to use any argument that has the slightest semblance of right, and they blow it up so much and deck it out so elaborately that the law tilts to their side and assigns them the property with a title so secure that it will stand firm beyond question or dispute. Again, if a man covets a castle, town, province, or other great estate, he applies so many bribes or pressures through friendships or other means that the property is taken from its owner and assigned to him, letters patent and the prince's seal attesting the legality and uprightness of the transaction.

This sort of thing happens also in ordinary business. Someone slyly loosens something from another's grasp, and the victim gazes helplessly after the culprit as he disappears with it around a corner. Or seeing a chance of perhaps making a profit—for example, at the expense of someone in trouble or debt who can neither hold on to his property nor avoid a loss if he sells—he hurries and pressures his victim until he has taken over half of his property or more; and yet this is considered an honest acquisition, not highway robbery or fraud. Hence the sayings, "First come, first served" and "Grab yours while you have the chance" and let the next man take what's left. Who is clever enough to imagine the vast amounts one could get by such pretty pretenses of fair business dealing? The world, however, does not consider such practices wrong. It does not see that these are ways of taking advantage of the neighbor and forcing him to sacrifice what he cannot spare without being hurt. Yet no one wants others to do such things to him. From this it is clear that all these shifts and shams are hypocritical.

Such wiles were also used in ancient times in respect to wives. Men used tricks such as this: If a man took a liking to another man's wife, he would manage in any one of a number of easily imagined ways, either personally or through others, to make her husband displeased with her, or he would have the wife antagonize her husband and make life so difficult for him that he was forced to dismiss her and give her up to the other man. Things of this sort no doubt happened often under the Jewish law. We even read in the Gospels that King Herod took his brother's wife while the latter was yet alive and that he nevertheless wanted to be regarded as an honorable, upright man, as St. Mark testifies. But I trust that such instances will not occur among us—though it could happen that a rich bride-to-be is enticed away from her commitment by trickery—because in the New Testament the married are forbidden to divorce each other. But what is not uncommon among us is that a person will lure away or alienate employees from their employers or otherwise estrange them with smooth-tongued words.

Be these things as they may, you must realize that God does not want you to deprive your neighbor of anything that is his by making him suffer loss while you fatten your greed. Even though in the world's view you may honorably keep the property, for you do to so is underhanded rascality and, as the saying goes, done by "sleight of hand" to escape detection. For although you may go about as if you had not wronged anyone, you nevertheless infringed on your neighbor's rights. People may not call it theft or fraud, yet it was a case of coveting your neighbor's property, that is, having designs upon it, diverting it from him against his will, and begrudging him what had been given to him by God. The judge, and everyone else, may have to allow it, but not God, for He sees the rascality of your heart and the trickery of the world. Give the world an inch, and it will take a yard. The resulting outcome is barefaced injustice and open violence.

Therefore let the ordinary meaning of these commandments stand. We are here forbidden to wish our neighbor's harm, to contribute to it, or to give occasion for it. If he has property, we are to be glad about it, allow him to enjoy it, and promote and protect everything that may be of service and profit to him, as we would wish him to do for us. Thus God has aimed these commandments especially against jealousy and miserable avarice, his purpose being to eradicate the roots and causes from which spring the things by which we injure our neighbor. Therefore He puts it clearly, in these words, "You shall not covet," etc. For, above all, He wants our hearts to be pure. However, as long as we live we will never be able to attain that standard. Thus, like all the other commandments, this commandment, too, constantly accuses us and shows us what our righteousness really amounts to in the sight of God.

### Conclusion of the Ten Commandments

Here in the Ten Commandments we have, then, a summary of divine teaching as to what we are to do in order that our whole life may please God. They are the true fountain and channel from which all that is to qualify as good works must spring and flow. Apart from the Ten Commandments no deed or conduct can be good or pleasing to God, however great or valuable it may be in the eyes of the world.

Let us then see what those great saints of ours find to boast about in their holy orders and in the great, arduous labors they have invented and set up to the neglect of the commandments, as if these were much too insignificant for our attention or as if they had already long since been fulfilled.

I should think that we would have our hands full trying to keep these commandments and to practice gentleness, patience and love toward enemies, chastity, kindness, and so on, together with everything else connected with these virtues. In the eyes of the world, however, works of this kind do not count for much and make little impression. For they lack novelty and pomp and are not bound to special times, places, rites, and ceremonies. They are rather the common, everyday domestic duties that one neighbor can render to another; for this reason they are given no recognition.

Those other works, however, dazzle the eyes and echo in the ears, aided by ceremonial pomp, costly splendor, and magnificent architecture for the production of a gleaming, glittering display. There is the smoke rising from swinging censers, the chanting, the jingling of bells, the lighting of tapers and candles, so that one can see or hear nothing else. For a priest to stand in a gold-embroidered chasuble or for a layman to be all day long on his knees in a church—things such as these are regarded as precious works that cannot be applauded enough. But for a poor girl to tend a little child and to do faithfully what she is told, that is regarded as nothing. Or why else would monks and nuns go into cloisters?

Look, isn't it devilish gall on the part of those desperate saints to presume to find a higher and better way of life than is taught in the Ten Commandments? They pretend, as we have said, that life according to the Ten Commandments is simplistic and therefore suited to the ordinary man, while theirs is a way of life for the saintly and the perfect. They do not see, these miserably blind people, that nobody can ever reach the point where he keeps even one of the Ten Commandments as it is meant to be kept. In fact, if we are to keep them, both the Creed and the Lord's Prayer must come to our aid, as we shall hear. Through them we are to strive for, pray for, and continuously receive the help we need for keeping the commandments. Thus the boasting of these saints is the same as if I would boast and say, "Of course I do not have a single dime toward payment of this bill, but I think that I can easily pay ten dollars."

I keep saying and stressing this so that people might give up the deeply rooted wretched abuses in which everyone is still enmeshed and so that people of all classes everywhere on earth may look only to the Ten Commandments and be concerned to follow their directives. It will be a very long time before men introduce a doctrine or a social order that matches up to the Ten Commandments, the demands of which are so high that no one can fulfill them by mere human strength. He who does fulfill them has to be a heavenly, angelic person, far above all the holiness of the world. Focus on them, really test yourself, apply all the strength and ability you have, and you then will really find so much to work at that you will not look for nor pay attention to any other works or types of holiness.

Let this suffice concerning what is to be learned and taught in Part One of the Catechism. In conclusion we must, however, repeat the text already dealt with under the First Commandment, in order to show how much effort God wants us to apply toward learning how to follow and practice the Ten Commandments.

*"I the Lord your God am a jealous God, visiting the iniquity of the fathers upon the children to the third and fourth generation of those who hate Me, but showing steadfast love to thousands of those who love Me and keep My commandments."*

Although, as we heard above, this appendix is attached primarily to the First Commandment, it was meant to apply to all the commandments. Collectively they all relate to it, and they should all be focused toward it. That is why I said that it should be kept before the young and impressed on them so that they learn and remember it and understand what it is that should urge and constrain us to keep the Ten Commandments. We should think of this appendix as being attached to each individual commandment, penetrating and permeating all of them.

As stated earlier, included in the words of this appendix is both a threat of wrath to terrify and warn us and a friendly promise to attract us and to beckon to us to take in and prize

God's words of command as being of divine seriousness. For He Himself here declares how intensely He is concerned about these commandments and how strictly He will watch for our observance of them. He points out how fearfully and terribly He will punish all who scorn and violate them, and again how richly He will reward, bless, and grant all manner of good things to those who value them highly and gladly live and act according to them. Thus He requires that all our actions should proceed from a heart that reverently fears God and looks to Him alone, and because of such reverent fear avoids everything that is against His will lest He be angered. Conversely, He demands a heart that trusts only in Him and for love of Him does what He wants because He proves Himself to be such a kind father and offers us His every grace and blessing.

Precisely this is also the sense and right interpretation of the first and chief commandment, the fountainhead of all the other commandments. Thus this word, "You shall have no other gods" intends to express very simply the same thing that is here demanded in the appendix: "You shall fear, love, and trust Me as your one true God." For he who has such an attitude of heart toward God has fulfilled this and all the other commandments. On the other hand, the person who fears and loves anything else in heaven or on earth will keep neither this nor any other commandment. Scripture has preached and urged this commandment everywhere, focusing everything on these two elements, fear of God and trust in God. The prophet David in particular does this throughout the Psalter, as when he says in Psalm 147:11: "The Lord takes pleasure in them that fear Him, in those that hope in His mercy." It is as if the whole commandment were unfolded in this single passage, as much as to say, "The Lord takes pleasure in those who have no other gods."

Thus the First Commandment is to illumine all the others and share its splendor with them. In order that it may be constantly repeated and never forgotten, let it run through all the commandments like the wire frame or hoop that runs through a wreath, joining the end to the beginning and holding everything together. For example, in the Second Commandment we are told to fear God and not misuse His name by cursing, lying, deceiving, or other kinds of wickedness and rascality; instead, we are to use it properly and worthily, addressing God in the prayer, praise, and thanksgiving that flow from the love and trust created in the image of the First

Commandment. Such fear, love, and trust in Him should drive us and draw us not to despise His Word, but learn it, hear it gladly, keep it holy, and honor it.

When we proceed to those commandments that involve our neighbor, the same holds true: everything stems from the force of the First Commandment. Thus we are to honor, be subject to, and obey father, mother, masters, and all authorities, not just for their sake but on account of God. You dare not inordinately respect or fear those who have such parental authority over you, doing or omitting to do something merely to please them; rather, pay attention to what God expects of you and will surely require of you. If you fail to do that, He will be your angry Judge, but otherwise your gracious Father.

Similarly, you are to do your neighbor no harm, injury, or violence, nor are you in any way to overstep the bounds as regards his person, spouse, property, honor, or rights as these are dealt with individually and in that order by the commandments, even though you have opportunity and a motive and nobody would blame you for doing so. On the contrary, you are to do good to all, helping them and promoting their interests however and whenever you can, purely out of love to God and in order to please Him in the confidence that He will richly repay it all. You see, then, how the First Commandment is the fountainhead and source of what flows through all the rest; to it they all again return as to the source upon which they all depend, for here in this First Commandment the end and the beginning are firmly looped and linked together.

It is helpful and necessary always to instruct, encourage, and remind young people concerning these things, so that they may be brought up not just with blows and coercion like cattle, but in the fear and reverence of God. These directions are not human trifles, but the commandments of the most high God. He watches over them with great and earnest care, and His wrath flames out to punish those who disdain them. On the other hand, He lavishly rewards those who keep them. Where people ponder this and take it to heart, there the urge and impulse gladly to do the will of God will arise spontaneously.

Not for nothing, therefore, did the Old Testament command men to write the Ten Commandments on every wall and in every corner, yes, even on their garments. The purpose was not simply to have them written there for display, as was the manner of the Jews. Rather, we are to keep them steadily before our eyes and constantly in our memories, and we are to put them into practice in all our actions and within our personalities. Everyone is to make them his habitual concern in every circumstance and in all his doings and dealings, as if they were written everywhere wherever he looks, yes, even wherever he walks and wherever he stands. Then he would find reminders enough, both for his private conduct at home and for his conduct out among his neighbors, to keep following the Ten Commandments, and nobody would need to go searching far and wide to find out what is right or wrong.

From all this we see once again how highly these commandments are to be praised and exalted above all orders, rules of conduct, and modes of behavior taught and practiced apart from them. Here we can boldly throw out the challenge: Let all the wise and good people step forward and show if they can produce a single work like those that God so earnestly calls for in these commandments. He requires, under threat of His high wrath and punishment, that they be obeyed, while at the same time adding the glorious promise that He will lavish all His gifts and blessings on us if we obey. We should therefore prize and value these commandments above all other teaching and regard them as the greatest treasure given to us by God.

## Second Part

### THE CREED

So far we have heard the first part of Christian teaching and seen in it everything God wants us to do and not to do. What properly follows is the Creed, which sets before us everything for which we must look to God and which we must receive as His gift. Briefly stated, the Creed teaches us to know thoroughly what He is like. And learning this is precisely what then is to enable us to do what we should be doing according to the Ten Commandments. For, as was stated above, their demands are set so high that all of man's power is much too feeble and weak to enable him to fulfill them. Therefore it is as essential to learn this second part of Christian teaching as it is to learn the former, in order that we may know how to reach our goal and where and through what means to find the power to keep the commandments. If by our own strength we were able to keep the Ten Commandments as they are meant to be kept, we would need nothing else, neither the teachings of the Creed nor of the Lord's Prayer. But before the usefulness and necessity of the Creed are explained it will, to begin with, be enough for the very simple to learn to understand the meaning of the Creed itself.

In the first place, the Creed was once divided into 12 articles. However, if one were to state separately all the teachings that are in the Scriptures and belong to the faith, there would be many more articles, not all of which could be as clearly and briefly expressed as are these in the Creed. But in order to organize them in as clear and simple a way as possible for the instruction of children, we shall summarize the entire Christian faith in three chief articles, according to the three persons in the Godhead, on whom everything that we believe is focused. Thus the First Article, of God the Father, sets forth creation; the Second, of God the Son, redemption; the Third, of God the Holy Spirit, sanctification. The Creed might be summed up very briefly in these few words: "I believe in God the Father, who created me; I believe in God the Son, who redeemed me; I believe in God the Holy Spirit, who sanctifies me." One God and one faith, yet three persons, and hence also three articles or confessions of faith. These we shall now briefly discuss.

### The First Article

*"I believe in God the Father Almighty, Maker of heaven and earth."*

This article very briefly describes the nature, will, activity, and work of God the Father. For since the Ten Commandments declared that we are to have only the one God, someone might ask, "What sort of person is God? What does He do? How can one praise or picture or describe Him in a way that will really let people know Him?" This article and the next two give the answer. Thus the Creed is nothing else than what Christians, when they respond to such questions, will reply and confess on the basis of the First Commandment. If, for example, one were to ask a young child, "My boy, what kind of God do you have? What do you know about Him?" then he could say, "First, my God is the Father who made heaven and earth. I take nothing and no one else as God except Him alone, for there simply is no one else who could have made heaven and earth."

However, for the somewhat more advanced and educated one could greatly expand the explanation of each of the three articles, dividing each one into as many parts as it has words. But for young pupils it is enough to point out the essential point in each, for example, as already stated, that the first article concerns the creation. We should stress the phrase, "Maker of heaven and earth." When you say, "I believe in God the Father Almighty, Maker," etc., what is it that you are saying? What do you mean by those words? Answer: "What I mean to say and what I believe is that I am a creation of God, that is, He gave me and continuously preserves for me my body, soul, and life, my bodily members great and small, all my senses, my reason and intellect, and so on, also food and drink, clothing, livelihood, wife and child, servants, house and home, etc.; besides this He causes the necessities and comforts of life to be provided for me by everything in creation—the sun, the moon, the stars in the sky, day and night, air, fire, water, the earth and all that it can produce, birds, fish, animals, grains and all manner of produce. He also gives whatever other physical and temporal blessings there may be, such as good government, peace, security." Thus we learn from this article that no one of himself obtained or could by himself preserve his life or any of the things that have been mentioned or could still be added, no matter how small and unimportant. All this is included in the word "Creator."

In addition, we also confess that God the Father not only gave us all that we have and see before our eyes, but He also daily protects and defends us against all evil and misfortune, turning aside danger and mishap of every sort. All this He does out of pure love and goodness, without our deserving it, like a kind father who takes care of us so that no harm may touch us. Anything further on this subject belongs in the other two parts of this article, where we say "Father" and "Almighty."

It follows self-evidently that, since everything that we possess as well as everything else in heaven and on earth is daily given, sustained, and preserved by God, therefore we in turn certainly owe it to Him to love, praise, and thank Him without ceasing and, in short, to serve Him wholly and completely, as He requires and enjoins us to do in the Ten Commandments.

It would take many words to describe in detail how few there are who believe this article. For all of us skim over it, hear it, and recite it without recognizing and considering what duty and privilege this article lays upon us. If we could believe it with our whole heart, then we would also act accordingly and would not so proudly strut about, insolently pluming ourselves as though we ourselves had produced our life, wealth, power, honor, and the like, and as though others must therefore fear and serve us. This is the world's perverse, wicked way; drowned in its blindness, it misused all the good gifts of God solely to serve its pride, greed, pleasure, and enjoyment, not even giving God so much as a thought, a word of thanks, or an acknowledgement that He is Lord and Creator.

Therefore this article, if we really believed it, would humble and terrify us. For we sin daily with our eyes, ears, hands, body and soul, money and property, and everything that we have. Those especially are guilty of doing this who still oppose the Word of God. Christians, however, have the advantage of at least recognizing their obligation to serve and obey God in response to all His kindness.

We should therefore daily work at this article and impress it on ourselves. We should remind ourselves of it by means of everything good we see or experience. And every time we escape from distress or danger, we should realize that this is a gift and act of God. He does all this for us so that we may look into His fatherly heart and sense how boundlessly He loves us. That would warm our hearts, setting them aglow with thankfulness toward God and with the will to use all these good things to His praise and glory.

Such, very briefly, is the sense of this article. It is as much as ordinary people at first need to learn concerning what we have received from God and what we owe Him in return. It offers splendid insight, but more than that, a precious treasure. In it we see how the Father has given Himself to us together with everything of His making and how He most richly provides for us in this life, quite apart from all the other inexpressible eternal blessings showered on us through His Son and His Holy Spirit, as we shall hear.

### The Second Article

*"And in Jesus Christ, His only Son, our Lord, who was conceived by the Holy Ghost, born of the Virgin Mary, suffered under Pontius Pilate, was crucified, dead, and buried; He descended into Hell; the third day He rose again from the dead; He ascended into heaven, and sitteth on the right hand of God the Father Almighty; from thence He shall come to judge the quick and the dead."*

Here we learn to know the second person of the Godhead and get to see what God gives us over and above the temporal blessings mentioned before—how He has poured Himself out completely for us, not withholding anything of Himself from us. This article is a very rich and far-reaching one, but for a brief and simple treatment, we shall take only one of its phrases and by means of it lay hold on the entire substance of this article. With the purpose of learning how we were redeemed, we shall here focus on these words, "in Jesus Christ, our Lord."

Now, when you are asked, "What do you believe according to the Second Article concerning Jesus Christ," answer very briefly, "I believe that Jesus Christ, the true Son of God, has become my Lord." What is it to "become my Lord"? This means He has redeemed me from sin, from the devil, from death, and from all evil. Before that, I had no Lord and King, but was held captive in the devil's power, condemned to die, and bound up in sin and blindness.

For when we had been created and had received all manner of good things from God the Father, the devil came and brought us down into disobedience, sin, death, and every misery. There we lay in disgrace with God and under His wrath, sentenced to the eternal damnation which we had brought on ourselves and thoroughly deserved. For us there was no counsel, help, or comfort until the one eternal Son of God in His boundless mercy pitied our misery and wretchedness and came from heaven to help us. All those former tyrant jailers have now been routed. Into their place stepped Jesus Christ, the Lord of life, righteousness, and every goodness and blessing, who has rescued us poor, lost humans out of the jaws of hell, won us, freed us, and brought us back into our Father's favor and grace; He has taken us beneath His shield and shelter to reign in us with His righteousness, wisdom, power, life, and bliss.

Let this article, then, be summarized in this way: the little word "Lord" simply means as much as Redeemer, that is, the One who rescued us from the devil to bring us to God, from death to bring us into life, from sin to bring us into righteousness, and now keeps us safe where He has brought us. The parts of this article that follow only explain and underscore the manner and the means by which the redemption came about, that is, how much it cost Christ, what He underwent, and what He risked in order to regain us and bring us back under his rulership. They declare that in order to conquer sin He became man, conceived and born without sin of the Holy Ghost and the Virgin Mary, that He suffered, died, and was buried in order to make satisfaction in my stead and pay what I owed, not with silver or gold, but with His own precious blood. All this He did in order to become my Lord. For He did none of this for Himself, nor did He need to. Then He rose again from the dead, swallowed up and devoured death, and finally ascended into heaven and assumed rulership at the right hand of the Father. Thus the devil and all powers must be subject to Him and be under His feet until on the last day He will separate and sunder us completely from the wicked world, the devil, death, sin, etc.

Detailed explanations of all these individual points, however, does not belong in brief addresses to children, but in sermons spread throughout the entire year, especially at the times fixed for the consideration of each of the subjects in detail: the birth, the suffering and death, the resurrection, and the ascension of Christ, and so on.

The entire Gospel that we preach depends on our thorough grasp of this article. Upon it rests our entire salvation and joy, and it is so rich and inclusive that it will keep challenging our efforts to learn it.

### The Third Article

*"I believe in the Holy Ghost; the holy Christian church, the communion of saints; the forgiveness of sins; the resurrection of the body; and the life everlasting. Amen."*

As I have pointed out, I cannot give this article a better title than "Of Sanctification." This phrase expresses and represents the person of the Holy Spirit and also His office, namely, to make us holy. In this article we base everything on the term "Holy Spirit," because it is so concise that there is no alternative for it. Scripture mentions all sorts of other spirits, such as human spirits, heavenly spirits, and evil spirits. But only God's Spirit is called Holy Spirit, that is the One who made us holy and continues to make us holy. For as the Father is called Creator and the Son is called Redeemer, so also it is because of His work that the Holy Spirit is to be called a Sanctifier, a Holy-maker, one who makes persons holy.

How, then, is the work of making people holy accomplished? Answer: Just as the Son wins His dominion over us by His birth, death, resurrection, etc., so the Holy Spirit accomplishes His work of sanctification through the following means as presented in the Third Article, namely the community of the saints, or the Christian church, the forgiveness of sins, the resurrection of the body, and the life everlasting. Accordingly, He first leads us into His holy congregation, placing us into the arms of the church, where He preaches to us and brings us to Christ.

For neither you nor I could ever know anything about Christ or believe in Him and receive Him as our Lord if it were not first offered to us and laid on our hearts by the Holy Spirit through the preaching of the Gospel. The redemptive work has taken place and is finished, for Christ has purchased and won the treasure for us through His suffering, death, resurrection, etc. But if that saving action stays hidden and no one knows about it, then it would all be for nothing, wasted. In order that this treasure might not remain buried but be taken up and enjoyed, God has let the Word go forth and be proclaimed. In the Word He has given us His Holy Spirit to lay the treasure of redemption on our hearts and make it our very own. Thus to sanctify or make holy is nothing else than to bring us to Christ our Lord to receive this treasure, which we could never have obtained by ourselves.

So learn to understand this article most clearly. If you then are asked what you mean by the words, "I believe in the Holy Spirit," you will be able to say, "I believe that the Holy Spirit makes me holy, as His name indicates." How does He do this? In what manner? By what means? Answer: "Through the holy Christian church, the forgiveness of sins, the resurrection of the body, and the life everlasting." For in the first place, He has a very special community in the world, which is the mother that brings forth and bears every Christian through the Word of God. The Holy Spirit reveals and proclaims that Word; He uses it to shed His light into human hearts and set them aglow; He empowers them to grasp the Word, accept it, cling to it, and faithfully stay with it.

For where He does not cause the Word to be proclaimed and to be grasped as the living truth within the heart, all is lost, as was the case under the papacy. There faith was shoved completely under the bench, and no one recognized Christ as Lord nor the Holy Spirit as the One who makes people holy. That is, no one believed that Christ is our Lord in the sense that, without our doing or deserving a thing, He won this treasure and qualified us to be favorably received by the Father. What was the trouble? The Holy Spirit was not there to reveal and proclaim these truths. Instead, men and evil spirits there taught us to save ourselves and so obtain God's grace by our own works. So it was no Christian church. For where Christ is not preached, there is no Holy Spirit, creating, calling, and gathering the Christian church, outside of which no one can come to the Lord Christ.

This is enough for a summary of this article. But since various points in it are not altogether clear to ordinary people, we shall run through them as well.

The term holy Christian church is defined in the Creed as *"communionem sanctorum,"* the communion of saints. The two terms mean the same thing. In olden times the second phrase was not used, and its translation as "communion of saints" is poor and misleading. Idiomatically rendered, it would be expressed quite differently. For the word "ecclesia" properly means "assembly," for which meaning we are accustomed to use the term "church"; simple folk, however, do not understand "church" to mean a gathering of people but rather a consecrated building or structure. Yet the building ought to be called a church only because of the group of people that gathers there. For we who come together prepare and use a particular place and apply to the building the term which we use for our group. Thus the word "church" really means nothing else than an ordinary assembly. It is not originally a native word, but comes, like the word "ecclesia," from the Greek. In Greek the word for "church" is *kyria,* in Latin it is *curia.* In our mother tongue it should therefore be rendered "a Christian congregation or assembly," or, to use the best, clearest expression of all, "a holy Christian people."

Similarly, the word *communio,* which is connected with it, should not be translated "communion" but "community." It is nothing but an interpretive comment intended as an explanation of what the Christian church is. Some of our people who understood neither Latin nor our own tongue rendered it "communion of saints," although this term is not native among us. Idiomatically phrased, it ought to be "a community of saints," that is a community in which are nothing but saints, or more clearly expressed, "a holy community." I say this in order that the expression, which has become so firmly fixed in our usage that it can hardly be uprooted again, may at least be understood; it would seem next to heresy to alter a word of it.

The sense and substance of this phrasing is: I believe that

a holy little flock or community exists on earth consisting entirely of saints under one head, Christ. It is called together by the Holy Spirit into one faith, one mind, one understanding. It possesses a variety of gifts, yet is united in love without sect or schism. I too am a part, a member of it. I am a copartner, participating and sharing in all its blessings. I was brought to and incorporated in this community by the Holy Spirit through my hearing and my continuing to hear the Word of God, which is the first step for entering the Christian church. Previously, before we came to this point, we belonged completely to the devil and did not really know God or Christ at all. But now the Holy Spirit through the Word remains present in the holy community and with the Christian people until the last day. Through this community He gathers us; through it He proclaims and applies the Word by which He creates and multiplies sanctification in order that His community may grow in numbers and become strong in faith and in the fruits of faith, which are the Spirit's creation.

We further believe that in this Christian community we have forgiveness of sins, which is given to us through the holy sacraments and absolution as well as through all the comforting passages of the entire Gospel. Therefore everything that is to be taught concerning the sacraments, in fact all Gospel preaching and all the functions of the Christian community focus on the forgiveness of sins. There is continuous need for this forgiveness. For although God's grace has been won by Christ and although the Holy Spirit effects holiness within the fellowship of the Christian church through the Word of God, yet because we are weighted with the burden of our flesh, our fallen nature, we are never without sin.

It is on this account that everything in the Christian church is so arranged that we may daily come here and get total forgiveness through the Word and the Sacraments to comfort our consciences and lift our spirits as long as we live. What the Holy Spirit does for us is this: although we have sin, yet He orders things so that it cannot injure us because we are within the Christian community in which there is complete forgiveness of sins. It is complete because God forgives us and because we mutually forgive, bear with, and lift up one another.

But because outside of the Christian church there is no Gospel, there is no forgiveness there either, and sanctification is therefore an impossibility as well. Therefore those who aim to earn and merit holiness through their own works rather than receiving it through the Gospel and its forgiveness of sins have expelled and separated themselves from the Christian community.

Meanwhile, since holiness has begun and is daily growing, we are waiting for the day when our flesh will be executed and buried with all its uncleanness, only to come forth and arise in glory to a complete and perfect holiness in a new and everlasting life. For the present we are only partially pure and holy. The Holy Spirit must continue to do His work in us through His Word, daily applying forgiveness until we reach that life where forgiveness will no more be needed. There people will be completely pure and holy, full of goodness and righteousness. In their new immortal, glorified bodies, they will be rescued and totally free from sin, death, and every evil.

All this, then, is the office and function of the Holy Spirit, to begin holiness on earth and to increase it daily through the Christian church and the forgiveness of sins, these two. But when we have returned to dust, He will complete His work in a moment and maintain it in us forever by means of the last two parts of this article.

One of these, however, "resurrection of the flesh," is not well expressed in the vernacular. For when we hear the word "flesh," our thought goes no farther than the meat counter. The idiomatic expression would be "resurrection of the body" or "of the dead body." However, this point is not of very great importance, provided that the words are rightly understood.

This, then, is the article that must remain constantly in operation. For the creation lies in the past, and the redemption has been accomplished also, but the Holy Spirit is at work without intermission until the last day. It is for the unbroken continuation of this ongoing work that He has established His community on earth; through it He speaks all His Word and does all His work. For He has not yet finished gathering all His Christian people or dispensing the forgiveness of sins. We therefore put our trust in Him who daily draws us into this Christian community through the Word and gives, increases , and strengthens our faith by means of that Word and its forgiveness of our sins. Then, when everything is accomplished and we, having continued in His Word to the end, die to the world and all evil, He will finally make us perfectly and eternally holy. We are now waiting in faith for this to be accomplished by means of the Word.

Notice that in the Creed you have God's entire essence, His will, and His work depicted in sharpest detail and in very short yet richly significant words. All our wisdom is based on them—a wisdom active far above all human wisdom, thought, and reason. For although the entire world has most carefully sought to understand the nature, mind, and activity of God, it has had no success in this whatever. But here in the Creed it is all given to you in richest measure. For in these three articles God Himself has revealed and disclosed the deepest profundity of His fatherly heart, His sheer inexpressible love. He created us for the very purpose that He might redeem us and make us holy. And besides giving and entrusting to us everything in heaven and on earth, He has given us His Son and His Holy Spirit in order to bring us to Himself through them. For, as we explained earlier, we were totally unable to come to a recognition of the Father's favor and grace except through the Lord Christ, who is the mirroring image of the Father's heart. Without Christ we see nothing in God but an angry and terrible Judge. But we could know nothing of Christ either, if it were not revealed to us by the Holy Spirit.

Accordingly, these articles of the Creed divide and distinguish us Christians from all other people on earth. All those outside of the Christian community, be they heathen, Turks, Jews, or false Christians and hypocrites, even though they believe in and worship only the one true God, nevertheless do not know how He is disposed toward them. They cannot confidently look toward Him for His love and blessing. Consequently, they remain in eternal wrath and damnation; for they do not have the Lord Christ nor are they enlightened and blessed by the Holy Spirit's gifts.

You see from this that the Creed is a very different teaching than the Ten Commandments. The Commandments did indeed teach us what we should be doing, but the Creed tells us what God does for us and what He gives to us. In any case, the Ten Commandments are written into every human heart, but the Creed no human wisdom is able to comprehend—it can be taught only by the Holy Spirit. Therefore the former teaching, that of the Ten Commandments, does not by itself make anyone a Christian; for the wrath and displeasure of God still remains upon us because what He requires of us we are unable to do. But this other teaching, that of the Creed, brings us sheer grace; and it makes us upright and pleasing to God because through this knowledge we get to love and delight in all the commandments of God. This is because we see in the Creed how God gives Himself together with all His gifts and powers to us for our help and support in keeping the Ten Commandments—with the Father giving us all created things, Christ giving us all His redemptive work, and the Holy Spirit giving us all His sanctifying gifts.

Let this suffice concerning the Creed for our present purpose of giving plain people the basics without overburdening them. Then, when they have understood the substance of the Creed, they can advance further by relating to these Catechism teachings whatever they learn in addition from Scripture, and thus they can constantly increase and enrich their understanding. On the subject of Christian faith we shall certainly have enough to preach and to learn daily for as long as we live.

## Third Part

## THE LORD'S PRAYER

Up to this point we have heard what we are to do and what we are to believe. In these two things consists the best and most blessed life. Now follows the third part, on how we are to pray. Our situation is such that no human being can keep the Ten Commandments perfectly, even though he has come to faith. Moreover, the devil, together with the world and our own flesh, resists with all his might our efforts to obey. Therefore nothing is so needful as to call upon God constantly and to din our plea into God's ear that He would give, preserve, and increase in us faith, and thus obedience to the Ten Commandments, and that He would clear away everything that stands in the way and is a hindrance to our obedience. In order that we might know what to pray for and how to pray, the Lord Christ Himself, as we shall see, has taught us both the manner in which and the words with which to pray.

But before we explain the petitions of the Lord's Prayer in sequence, it is probably more necessary to exhort and encourage people to pray as also Christ and His apostles did. First, we must know that it is our duty to pray because prayer is commanded by God. As we have heard in the Second Comandment: "Thou shalt not take the name of the

Lord, thy God, in vain." What this commandment requires of us is to praise the holy name and to pray or call upon it in every need. For calling upon God's name is nothing else than praying. In this commandment we are therefore as strictly and solemnly commanded to pray as in the others we are commanded not to have any other God, not to kill, not to steal, etc. Let no one imagine that it is all the same whether I pray or do not pray, as the crude-minded imagine who go on thinking, "Why should I pray? Who knows whether God pays attention to my prayer or wants to listen? If I do not pray, there will always be someone else who does." So they fall into the habit of never praying, excusing their neglect with the false allegation that since we reject false and hypocritical praying, we teach that one ought not or need not pray at all.

It is true that the babbling and droning in church that used to be taken for prayer was of course no real praying. Such external repetition, properly used, may be good exercise for children, pupils, and plain folk; it might be called singing or reading, but genuine prayer is not the term for it. As the Second Commandment teaches, to pray is to "call upon God in every trouble." It is this that He requires of us, and He does not leave it up to our own choice. Rather, if we want to be Christians, we should and must pray, just as we must be obedient to father, mother, and government. For by calling on God in prayer, we honor His name and use it purposefully. Let us, by all means, take note of this in order to silence and repel any thoughts that would deter or discourage us from praying. For a son to say to his father, "What's the use of obeying? I'll go and do as I please. And why not? What difference does it make?" is wasted breath; for there stands the commandment, "You shall and must obey." Similarly, whether to pray or not is not left to my choice, but I am required and in duty bound to pray or else incur the wrath and displeasure of God.

This we should take hold of and remember above all things so that we may thereby silence and thrust from us the thoughts that would deter or discourage us from praying, as though it did not matter much whether we pray or not, or as though to pray is commanded to those who are holier or in a better relationship with God than we are. The human heart is indeed by nature so perverse that it is always in flight from God, imagining that He does not want or care about our prayer because we are sinners and deserve nothing but His wrath. To counteract such thinking, we should heed this commandment and turn to God, so that we may not anger Him even more by continuing to disobey it. He makes it amply clear in this commandment that He does not want to cast us out or drive us away, even though we are sinners, but on the contrary wishes to draw us to Himself, so that we may humble ourselves before Him, confess our misery and trouble, and pray for mercy and help. Thus we read in Scripture that He is angry because those who were punished for their sins did not turn back to Him and did not soften His wrath and seek His grace by prayer.

From the stress God lays upon His command to pray, we ought to conclude that on no account should anyone neglect his prayers, but he should rather prize them and make much of them. Let the other commandments serve as an illustration. A child should under no circumstances despise obedience to father and mother, but always think, "This is a work of obedience which I do for no other purpose than to act in agreement with my duty and the command of God. On this firm base I can take my stand and think highly of my act of obedience, not on account of any merit in me but on account of the commandment of God." So also here. We should look upon the form and the substance of our prayers as something God has demanded and we are doing in obedience to Him. We should think of it like this: "On my account the prayer would be worth nothing; yet it does have great value because God commanded it." So, in obedience to this commandment everyone should always present his prayers before God, no matter what it is that he needs to pray for.

We therefore beg and diligently exhort everyone to take these things to heart and under no circumstances to disdain prayer. Prayer used to be taught in the name of the devil in such a way that no one regarded it as anything special; people thought it was enough if one went through the mere motions of prayer, regardless of whether God was listening or not. That is gambling with prayer and mumbling by rote on the off-chance of being heard. Such praying is worthless.

We allow ourselves to be led astray and turned off by such thoughts as these: "I am not holy enough or worthy enough to pray. If I were as godly and flawless as St. Peter and St. Paul, then I would pray." Away with such thoughts! For exactly the same commandment applies to St. Paul and to me; the Second Commandment was issued just as much for my sake as for his. He cannot boast of having any better or holier commandment than I have.

What you therefore should say is this: "The prayer I offer is just as precious, holy, and pleasing to God as that of St. Paul and the holiest of the saints. How so? Well, I gladly admit that he is holier as regards his person, but not as regards the commandment. For God regards the prayer not on account of the person, but on account of His own Word and the obedience to that Word. Upon the same commandment on which the saints base their prayers, I base mine, too; besides, I pray for precisely the same things for which all of them pray or have ever prayed."

The first and most necessary point is this, that all our prayers be founded and fixed upon obedience to God, regardless of our person, whether we are full of sin or upright, worthy or unworthy. And we should know that God will not have this commandment taken as a jest but will punish us in His wrath if we fail to pray, just as He punishes all other disobedience. Nor will He let our prayers be useless or wasted. For if He did not intend to hear you, He would not have told you to pray nor nailed His words down with such a strict commandment.

In the second place, we should all the more be impelled and encouraged to pray because God has also added the promise that our prayers will surely be answered, as He says in Psalm 50:15, "Call upon Me in the day of trouble; I will deliver you," and as Christ says in the Gospel of Matthew 7:7-8, "Ask, and it will be given you," etc. "For every one who asks receives." Promises such as these certainly ought to awaken delight in our hearts and kindle in them the love to pray. For God by His Word testifies that our prayers heartily please Him and will definitely be heard and granted. This He does so that we may not disdain His promise or cast it to the wind or pray in uncertainty.

You can hold Him to His promises and say, "I come to you, dear Father, and pray not of my own accord or in my own worthiness, but because of Your command and Your promises, which cannot fail me nor mislead me." Whoever does not believe His promises should once again realize that he provokes God's wrath by grossly dishonoring Him and accusing Him of lying.

We should be all the more encouraged and induced to pray by the fact that, in addition to giving us His command and promise, God Himself takes the first step by supplying and putting into our mouths the words and pattern for the how and the what of our prayer life. He wants us to see how genuinely He is concerned about our needs, so that we may never question whether our prayers please Him or are really answered. This gives the Lord's Prayer a great advantage over all other prayers that we ourselves might devise. For in their case the conscience might constantly be in doubt and say, "I have prayed, but who knows if it pleases Him or whether I have hit upon the right measure or manner of praying?" Nowhere on earth, therefore, can a nobler prayer be found than the Lord's Prayer, since it gives such splendid testimony that God delights in hearing us pray. We should not wish to trade this assurance for all the world's riches.

The Lord prescribed this prayer with the aim of making us realize and ponder the needs that ought to impel and drive us to pray incessantly. A would-be petitioner must refer to, present, and name the things he is asking for; unless he does this, it cannot be called a prayer.

Therefore we have rightly rejected the kind of praying done by monks and priests who day and night wail and whimper fit to kill, yet not one of them thinks of asking even for a splinter of anything. If we brought together all their churches and all their clergy, they would have to confess that never did they really pray for as much as a drop of wine. Of not one of them could it be said that he determined to pray out of obedience to God and faith in His promise, or out of a sense of his need. At best they only thought of doing a good work by which to pay their dues to God, willing only to give Him something, not to receive anything from Him.

Where prayer is genuine, there must be earnestness. We must feel our need, the kind of pressure that drives us to cry aloud. Then prayer will arise by itself, as it should, and we will need no instruction on how to prepare for it or from what fountain to draw a spirit of devotion. The need that should concern us, both our own need and that of others, is indicated amply enough in the Lord's Prayer. This should serve to remind us and deeply impress upon us not to become slack in our prayer life. We all have more than enough needs, but our trouble is that we do not feel or see them. Hence God wants you to lament your needs and express your wants, not as though he did not know about them, but in order that your heart might kindle with stronger desires and more insistent and more frequent prayer requests, and that you then might simply open up and spread out your cloak to receive God's plenty.

Each of us from his youth up should form the habit of praying every day for all those needs of which he becomes conscious when something affects him or the people around him. We should pray for preachers, government officials, neighbors, employers. We should always, as stated before, remind God of His commandment and His promise, realizing that He will not allow them to be despised. I say this because I would so like these things to be again brought home to people, so that they would learn to pray rightly instead of carrying on in the raw, cold manner that makes them daily more clumsy at praying. That indeed is what the devil wants as he bends every effort to that end. For he well knows what harm and damage it does to him when prayer life flourishes.

We need to realize that prayer alone is our protecting shield and shelter. We are much too weak to cope by ourselves with the devil, his might, and the forces he has lined up against us. They could easily trample us under foot. Therefore we must be alert and grasp the weapons with which Christians should be armed in order to withstand the devil. How do you suppose that, except for the intervention of the prayers of a few godly men like a wall of iron, such great things were accomplished as the checking or frustration of our enemies' designs, plots, murders, and seditions by which the devil had intended to crush both us and the Gospel? Had it not been for these prayers, the enemies themselves would have witnessed a very different game and seen the devil destroying all Germany in her own blood. They may now be overconfidently laughing and mocking, but by prayer alone we shall continue to be a match both for them and for the devil, provided that we keep on praying diligently and do not relax. For when any good Christian prays, "Dear Father, Thy will be done," God in heaven answers, "Yes, dear child, it will most certainly be done despite the devil and the whole world."

By way of admonition let it be said that one should above all things learn to value prayer as something great and precious, clearly distinguishing between mere mumbling and really praying for something specific. We most definitely do not denounce prayer, only the totally useless blaring and bleating, as Christ Himself rejects and forbids long senseless repetitions.

We shall now proceed to treat the Lord's Prayer as briefly and clearly as possible. Here, in seven successive articles or petitions, all the needs that constantly beset us are gathered up, each one of which is so great that it ought to drive us to pray about it as long as we live.

## The First Petition

*"Hallowed be Thy name."*

These words are somewhat obscure and not really according to common usage. In our tongue we would normally say, "Heavenly Father, grant that Your name alone be holy." What are we praying for when we ask that His name may become holy? Is it not holy already? The answer is, Yes, of course, God's name is holy in itself, but in our use of it His name is not kept holy. The name of God was given to us when we became Christians and were baptized; consequently we are called God's children and possess the sacraments, through which God so incorporates us with Himself that everything that is His has to serve for our use.

It is therefore very necessary and should be our prime concern to give the name of God its due honor and to keep it holy and sacred, looking upon it as our greatest, most sacred treasure. As God's good children, we must pray that His name, which is holy in heaven whether we pray or not, may be kept holy on earth by us and by all the world.

How, then, is God's name kept holy among us? To answer as clearly as possible: When both what we teach and the way we live are godly and Christian. For since in this prayer we call God our Father, we have the duty to conduct ourselves in every situation as His good children, so that we may not be a disgrace to Him but bring Him honor and praise.

Now, the name of God may be dishonored either with words or with deeds; for all that we do on earth may be classified either as word or as deed, either as speech or as action. In the first place, then, the name of God is profaned by anyone who preaches, teaches, or speaks in God's name anything that is false and misleading, using His name to cover up a lie and make it seem credible. This is the worst possible disgrace and dishonor to the name of God. God's name is also profaned when men grossly misuse it as a cover for their swearing, cursing, conjuring, etc. Next, it is also profaned by openly wicked lives and conduct, as when those who are called Christians and people of God are adulterers, drunkards, maggotty misers, envious persons, slanderers; here again the name of God becomes an object of scorn and blasphemy because of us.

It brings shame and disgrace on an earthly father to have

a child go bad and be antagonistic to him in speech and conduct, so that because of the child he must suffer contempt and ridicule. Just so also God is dishonored if we who bear the heavenly Father's name and have received all manner of blessing from Him teach, speak, or live otherwise than as godly children of His, with the result that He must hear people speak of us not as children of God but as children of the devil.

So you see that we pray in this petition for the very thing that God demands in His Second Commandment: that His name be not misused for swearing, cursing, lying, deceiving, etc., but that it be used for the good purpose of praising and honoring God. For whoever uses God's name in connection with any kind of wrong profanes and desecrates this holy name, as in the past a church was regarded as desecrated when murder or some other villainy had been committed there, or when a monstrance or a relic had been profaned, such misuses rendering unholy what in itself was holy. Thus this petition is plain and clear once the expression "to hallow" is understood to mean the same as our idiomatic terms "to glorify, to praise, to honor" by speech or conduct.

Note, then, the great need for this kind of petition. We can see how full of sects and false teachers the world is, all of them using the divine name as a disguise and cover-up for their devilish doctrine. This should certainly cause us incessantly to call out and complain to God about all such who preach and believe falsely, and about those who attack and persecute our Gospel and pure doctrine and try to smother it, as do the bishops, tyrants, fanatics, and the like. This petition is directed also against us who have the Gospel but are not thankful for it nor live according to it as we should.

If you pray this petition from the heart, you can be sure that it pleases God. There is nothing dearer to Him than to hear His praise and glory exalted above everything else and His Word taught in its purity and highly valued and treasured.

### The Second Petition

*"Thy kingdom come."*

We prayed in the first petition that God would hinder the world from cloaking its lies and wickedness with the glory and name of God, and also that we might keep His name holy and sacred both in doctrine and in life, so that God might be

85

glorified and praised on account of us. Similarly, we pray here in the second petition that His kingdom may come. But just as God's name is holy in itself and we nevertheless pray that it may be holy among us, so also the kingdom of God comes of itself without our prayer, and yet we pray that it may come to us. That is, we ask for God to be active in us and among us, so that we may be part of the people among whom His name is revered and His rule is flourishing.

What is the kingdom of God? Answer: Nothing else than what we heard above in the Creed, namely that God sent His Son, our Lord Christ, into the world to redeem us and set us free from the power of the devil and to bring us to Himself and rule over us as a king of righteousness, life, and salvation in defiance of sin, death, and an evil conscience; that He also gave us His Holy Spirit in order to bring these truths home to us through His holy Word and to enlighten us and strengthen faith in us by His power.

Therefore we pray here at the outset that all this may take vigorous root in us and that God's name may be glorified through His holy word and our Christian lives. We ask for this both in order that we who have accepted it may stay with it and daily grow in it, and that other people also may be attracted and become attached to it and that it may move forward with power through the earth. Thus it is our prayer that through the leading of the Holy Spirit many may come into the kingdom of grace and share salvation with us, so that together we may continue forever in the kingdom that has now begun among us.

The coming of God's reign takes place in two ways. First, on earth, here in time, it comes through the Word and through faith in the Word. Then, secondly, in eternity, it comes through the final revelation of our Lord at His return. We pray that both of these aspects of the Kingdom may come: on the one hand, that the Kingdom may come to those who are not yet in it; on the other hand, that to us who have already attained it, it may come by way of perpetual growth both here in our daily life and hereafter in eternal life. All this is the same as saying, "Dear Father, give us, we pray, Your Word, so that the Gospel may be genuinely preached throughout the world. And grant that it be accepted by faith and be alive and do its work in us, so that Your reign may flourish among us through the Word and power of the Holy Spirit and that the devil's reign may be overthrown and have no claim or power over us, until finally it is totally destroyed and we live forever in perfect righteousness and blessedness."

From this you can see that we are here not asking for a bit of a handout or for temporal, transitory blessings, but for a priceless eternal treasure and for everything that belongs to God Himself. The treasure is far too great for a human being to dare to take it into his head to desire it if God Himself had not commanded us to pray for it. But because He is God, He wants the honor of giving us many more gifts and much richer ones than anyone can comprehend. For He is an eternally unchangeable fountain which, the more it gushes forth and overflows, the more it gives of itself. There is nothing greater that He desires of us than that we ask Him for many and great things; conversely, it angers Him if we do not ask confidently and make great demands on Him.

Suppose that the richest and mightiest emperor on earth were to order a poor beggar to ask for whatever his heart might desire and were prepared to give him great imperial gifts. And suppose that the fool of a beggar would ask for no more than a ladle of beggar's soup. For having treated his imperial majesty's command with mockery and contempt, he would rightly be regarded as a rogue and a scoundrel and as one who was not worthy ever again to come into the emperor's presence. It similarly exposes God to shame and disgrace if we to whom He offers and assures so many inexpressible riches despise them or do not confidently expect to receive them, but instead are scarcely able to bring ourselves to ask for a piece of bread.

The blame for all this rests on shameful unbelief, which does not even trust God for enough to fill the belly, let alone expect, without doubting, to receive the eternal treasures from Him. We must therefore strengthen ourselves against unbelief and ask first of all for the great gifts of the kingdom of God. Then we will surely also have all the other things in rich supply, as Christ teaches, "Seek first His kingdom and His righteousness, and all these things shall be yours as well" (Matt. 6:33). For how could God let us suffer for want of temporal gifts when He promises to give us the eternal and imperishable treasure?

### The Third Petition

*"Thy will be done on earth as it is in heaven."*

So far we have prayed that God's name would be honored by us and His kingdom flourish among us. These two petitions include everything relative to God's glory and our salvation, in order that we might have God and all His riches as our very own. But here it becomes extremely necessary for us to hold on firmly to these treasures and never let ourselves be torn away from them. A good government not only needs those who build and govern well, but also defenders, protectors, and vigilant watchmen. So also here. When we have prayed for the foremost necessities, for the Gospel, for faith to accept it, and for the Holy Spirit to govern us who have been redeemed out of the devil's power, then we must furthermore pray that God's will be done. For it will strike us as very strange that, if while we are to hold on to those treasures, we must on their account suffer many attacks and assaults from all those who undertake to hinder and thwart what we ask for in the first two petitions.

No one is ready to believe how much the devil opposes and obstructs their fulfillment. He cannot stand having anyone teach or believe the right things. It torments him unspeakably to see his lies and atrocious deceptions, once honored under a most attractive semblance of God's name, exposed in all their shame to public view as he himself is driven out of human hearts and his kingdom is cracked wide open. Like a furiously angry foe he therefore rages and lashes out with all his venomous might, marshals all his underlings, and even enlists the aid of his allies, the world and our own flesh. For in itself our flesh is indolent and inclined to evil, even when we have accepted God's Word and believe it; as for the world, it is completely wicked and evil. The devil inflames these two, blowing and stirring the blaze in an effort to halt us, drive us back, overthrow us, and bring us again into his power. That is the one thought, desire, and purpose toward which he is straining day and night, resting not a wink and employing all the arts, tricks, means, and methods that he can possibly dream up.

We who want to be Christian must certainly expect and be prepared for having the devil, all his evil angels, and the world as our enemies. We must count on their causing us all manner of misfortune and heartache. For where God's Word is preached, accepted or believed, and bearing fruit, there the blessed holy cross will not be absent either. Let no one imagine that a Christian will have peace. Rather, he will have to risk everything that he has on earth, his possessions, honor, house and home, wife and child, life and limb. Now, our flesh, the old Adam, finds this to be most painful. For it means that we must hold steady and suffer patiently while

88

under attack, and that we must give up whatever is taken from us.

Therefore, the need is as great in these as in all other situations that we should pray without ceasing, "Dear Father, Your will be done, not the will of the devil and our enemies, nor the will of those who persecute and wish to stifle your Word or prevent the coming and progress of Your kingdom; and grant that we may patiently bear and overcome whatever we may have to suffer on account of Your Word and kingdom, lest our poor flesh retreat or surrender out of weakness or apathy."

Notice that these three petitions very simply express matters of concern to God Himself, and yet everything in them concerns us. What we pray for here does pertain to us, but only in the sense that we are asking for those things to be accomplished in us that in any case will be accomplished without us. For just as God's name shall be hallowed and His kingdom come without any prayer of ours, so also shall His will be done and prevail, even though the devil and all his forces storm, fume, and furiously rage against it in their effort utterly to eradicate the Gospel. But we must pray for our own sake that despite their fury God's will may have its way unhindered among us so that they can accomplish nothing. We must pray that in the face of powerful pressures and persecution we may stand firm and submit to whatever God's will permits to come upon us.

Such prayer, then, must be our offensive and defensive weapon to beat back and subdue whatever the devil, bishops, tyrants, and heretics attempt against the Gospel. Let them all rage in unison and try their worst in plotting and scheming how to stifle us and stamp us out in order that their will and their designs may prevail. One or two Christians armed with this one petition shall be our walled stronghold, against which our assailants shall dash themselves to pieces. Our solace and our boast is that the will and the purposes of the devil and all our foes must and shall go down in utter defeat and destruction, no matter how proudly secure and powerful they think themselves. For if their will would not be broken and baffled, the kingdom of God could not continue on earth nor could His name be hallowed.

### The Fourth Petition

*"Give us this day our daily bread."*
Here we now consider that poor breadbox, the needs of our

body and of our earthly life. It is a brief, plain word, this petition, but it covers a wide area. For when you pray for "daily bread," you are praying for everything that contributes to your having and enjoying your daily bread, and conversely you are praying against everything that would prevent you from having and enjoying it. So you must open up and expand your thinking, so that it reaches not only as far as the flour bin and baking oven but also out over the broad fields, the farmlands, and the entire country that produces, processes, and conveys to us our daily bread and all kinds of nourishment. For if God did not make crops to grow and did not bless and preserve them in the fields, we could never have a loaf of bread to take from the oven and put on the table.

Briefly stated, this petition is meant to include everything that is connected with our entire life on earth because it is only for the sake of this life that we need daily bread. Now, what we need in order to live is not only food, shelter, and other necessities for the body, but also peace and harmony between us and those among whom we live and move in our daily business, trade, or association of any kind—in short, we need everything that pertains to the management not only of our domestic but also of our community or civic affairs. For where these two, the domestic and civil relationships, are disrupted and do not function properly, there also the necessities of life are interfered with, until finally life itself cannot long be maintained. Probably the greatest need of all is for us to pray for our civil authorities and government. They are chiefly the ones through whom God preserves our daily bread and all the comforts of life. For although we have received from God an abundance of all good gifts, yet we cannot retain any of them or enjoy them in happy security unless God grants us a stable and peaceable government. For where there is strife, wrangling, and war, there our daily bread is already taken from us, or at least threatened.

Therefore, as a suitable emblem, one might well put a loaf of bread into the coat of arms of every worthy prince instead of a lion or a victory wreath emblem, or one might stamp it upon the coins of the realm, in order to remind both the princes and their subjects that it is a ruler's function to provide us with the protection and peace without which we could not steadily enjoy the blessing of daily bread. Rulers are therefore worthy of all honor, and we should fulfill our duties toward them and do for them what we can, since they are the ones who make it possible for us to enjoy what is ours in peace and quietness, and since without them we would not be able to keep a penny. We should pray for them, that through them God may bestow on us further blessing and good things.

Let us sketch very briefly how far this petition extends into all kinds of relationships on earth. A long prayer of many words could be made out of it by listing all the things it includes. For example, we could pray God to give us food and drink, clothing, house and home, a healthy body; to let the grain and the fruits of the field grow to maturity; to help us to manage our household affairs well; to give and preserve to us a good wife, good children, good servants; to cause our job, trade, or occupation to succeed and prosper; to send us good neighbors and good friends, and so on. We could continue our prayer by asking God to give wisdom, strength, and success to emperor and king and all authorities, particularly our governors, counselors, magistrates, and officials, enabling them to rule well and to be victorious over aggressors and all enemies; to enable their subjects and people in general to live together in obedience, peace, and harmony; on the other hand, to guard us against all manner of harm to our body and means of subsistence, against storm, hail, fire, and flood, against poison, pestilence, and cattle disease, against war and bloodshed, famine, savage beasts, wicked persons, and similar evils. It is well to impress on the people in general that all the above good things and others like them do come from God and must be prayed for.

But this petition is chiefly directed against our worst enemy, the devil. His sole intent and desire is to take from us the things that come to us from God or to interfere with their benefiting us. He is not satisfied to disrupt and destroy spiritual order so as to mislead souls with his lies and bring them under his power, but he also obstructs and hinders the establishment of any kind of order or honorable and peaceful human relations. So he causes endless strife, murders, riots, and war; also tempests and hail to destroy crops and cattle; also pollution of the atmosphere, and so on. In short, it pains him when he sees anyone receiving a bit of bread from God and eating it in peace. If it were in his power and if, next to God, our prayers did not restrain him, we would certainly not be able to keep one blade of vegetation in the field, one penny in the house, or even one hour of our life, especially if we belong to those who have God's Word and want to be Christians.

Notice the way God wants to show us how He cares for us in all our need and how faithfully He provides for our day by day existence. Although He gives these things and sustains them for us in rich supply, also in the case of wicked men and scoundrels, yet He wishes us to pray for these blessings, so that we may recognize that they come to us from His hand and, when we receive them, feel His fatherly goodness toward us. When He withdraws His hand, nothing can prosper or succeed for long, as we can easily see and experience day by day. What a plague everywhere in the world is counterfeit money, not to mention the wanton exploitation and the usurious interest rates in ordinary business, trade, and labor that are imposed by those who crush the poor and deprive them of their daily bread. This we must endure, it is true. But let the exploiters and oppressors beware of losing the intercession of the church, and let them take care that this petition of the Lord's Prayer does not turn against them.

### The Fifth Petition

*"And forgive us our trespasses as we forgive those who trespass against us."*

This petition is concerned with our poor, miserable conduct. Although we have the Word of God, believe in Him, obey Him, and submit to His will, and though His gifts and blessings nourish our lives, yet we do not live without sinning. Because we live in the world among people who sorely vex us and give us occasion for impatience, anger, revenge, and so on, we stumble every day and overstep our bounds. We also, as we have heard, have Satan coming up from behind to close in on every side and aim his attacks against all our earlier petitions. Amid such constant conflict, it is not possible always to stand firm.

Here again, therefore, the need is great for us to pray and to call upon God, "Dear Father, forgive us our trespasses." Not that He does not forgive sins without our prayer or before we ask. In fact, before we prayed for it or ever thought about it, He gave us the Gospel, in which there is nothing but forgiveness. But here the point is that we should recognize and accept this forgiveness. It is the way of the flesh, in which we live our daily life, to distrust and disbelieve God and to stir itself up constantly with evil desires and devices, so that we sin every day in word and deed, doing what is wrong and omitting to do what is right. As a result, our conscience feels unrest, fears God's wrath and displeasure, and thus lets the comfort and assurance of the Gospel sink low. Therefore it is necessary to keep running to the Gospel and drawing comfort from it by means of this petition in order to revive our good conscience.

This process, however, is to serve God's purpose, namely to break our pride and keep us in humility. For He has reserved the prerogative, in case anyone insists on his own goodness and despises others, to let him look into himself when this petition confronts him. He will find that he is no better than others and that in the presence of God everyone must duck his head and come into the joy of forgiveness only through the low door of humility. Let no one think that in this life he will ever reach the point where he does not need this forgiveness. In short, unless God keeps on forgiving us, we are lost.

Thus this petition is really an appeal to God not to rivet His eyes on our sins nor to punish them as we daily deserve, but to deal with us according to His grace and forgive us as He promised, and so to give us a happy and cheerful conscience able to stand before Him in prayer. Where the heart is not right with God and cannot draw such confidence from His Gospel, it will never dare to pray. But such a confident and joyful heart can come from nowhere else than from the knowledge that our sins are forgiven.

Meanwhile, a necessary yet comforting word is attached here: "as we forgive those who trespass against us."' God has promised us the certain assurance that all is completely forgiven and pardoned, yet with the understanding that we are also to forgive our neighbor. For just as God in His grace forgives everything by which we sin much against Him every day, so we also must constantly forgive our neighbor who does us harm, violence, and injustice, treats us with abominably shabby tricks, and the like. If you do not forgive, do not imagine that God will forgive you. But if you do forgive, you have the comfort and assurance that in heaven you are forgiven. But you are forgiven not on account of the forgiveness you granted to your neighbor, for God forgives completely and for nothing, out of pure grace and because He promised it, as the Gospel teaches. Rather, God has linked our forgiveness of our neighbor to God's forgiveness of us for our strengthening and assurance, and as a sign alongside the promise in Luke 6:37, which agrees with this petition, "Forgive, and you will be forgiven." Hence Christ repeats the promise immediately after the Lord's Prayer, Matthew 6:14, and says, "For if you forgive men their trespasses, your heavenly Father also will forgive you," etc.

Thus this sign is attached to the petition so that when we pray we might remember the promise and think, "Dear Father, I come to You pleading for Your forgiveness not because I make up for my sins or earn Your forgiveness with my act of forgiveness, but I come because You have promised forgiveness and attached the seal to it so as to make it as certain as if You had Yourself audibly spoken the absolution to me." For everything that Baptism and the Lord's Supper—externally appointed as signs—can accomplish, that also this sign can do for the strengthening and cheering of our conscience. It is a sign that we are privileged to use and practice every hour as our constant standby.

### The Sixth Petition

*"And lead us not into temptation."*

We have now heard enough about all the laborious effort needed to preserve and retain the many gifts we pray for. Yet in these efforts we will never manage to avoid flaws and missteps. Moreover, though we have received forgiveness and obtained a good conscience, having been fully absolved, yet life is such that one who is standing today falls tomorrow. Therefore, although at the present moment we stand upright and with a clear conscience before God, we must go on to pray that he will not allow us to fall, defeated by trials and temptations.

Temptation (or allurement, as the ancient Saxons called it) is of three kinds: by the flesh, the world, and the devil. We live in the flesh and carry the old Adam hanging around our necks; he is at work every day inciting us to unchastity, laziness, gluttony, and drunkenness, to greed and deceit-fulness, to acts of fraud and deception against our neighbor—in short, to all kinds of evil lusts that cling to our nature and to which we are stimulated by other people's company and example and by what we otherwise hear and see. All this often bruises and scorches even an innocent heart.

Next comes the world, which hurts us by word and deed, and drives us to anger and impatience. In short, one sees nothing in the world but hate and envy, enmity, violence and injustice, disloyalty, revenge, cursing, abuse, slander,

94

arrogance and pride, combined with excessive finery, flattery, fame, and power. No one is satisfied to be low on the ladder but wants to be at the top and visible to everyone.

Now comes the devil as well, harassing us and fuming at us from all sides, concentrating his attacks especially where conscience and spiritual matters are at stake. His chief aim is to make us discard both God's Word and His works, to tear us away from faith, hope, and love, to draw us into misbelief, false security, and stubborn impenitence, or else to drive us into despair, denial of God, blasphemy against Him, and countless other horrible sins. These are the devil's traps and nets, or more exactly, the most venomously poisoned "fiery darts" (Ephesians 6:16) which not flesh and blood but Satan shoots into our hearts.

These grave perils and great temptations, which every Christian must endure, are grievous even if they come singly one by one. They constrain us, as long as we remain in this wretched life, where we are pursued, hounded, and harried on all sides, to cry out and pray every hour that God would not allow us to become faint and weary and to fall back into sin, shame, and unbelief. Otherwise it is impossible to overcome even the very slightest temptation.

"Leading us not into temptation" consists of God giving us the power and strength to resist it even though the tribulation itself is not turned aside nor put to an end. For not one of us can successfully bypass temptations and enticements as long as we are living in the flesh and the devil is lurking about. Nothing else is to be expected than that we shall suffer trials and temptations, yes, even find ourselves bogged in them. However, what we pray for here is that we may not fall down into them and be drowned.

It is a very different thing to feel a temptation than to submit and say yes to it. All of us are bound to feel temptations, though not all to the same degree; some have more and stronger temptations than others. For example, the young are chiefly tempted by the flesh, older people by the world, and those others who are involved with spiritual matters—that is, strong Christians—by the devil. But merely feeling a temptation, as long as it is against our will and we would rather be rid of it, cannot harm us. For if the temptation were not felt, it could not be called temptation at all. But yielding to temptation is a matter of giving it free rein, not resisting it, not praying for help against it.

We Christians must therefore keep ourselves well armed,

always expecting to be under incessant attack. None of us dare carelessly go about in a false sense of security as if the devil were far away. Instead, wherever we are, we should expect his blows and be ready to ward them off. Even if at the moment I am chaste, patient, kindly, and stand firm in the faith, yet this very hour the devil is likely to drive such a shaft into my heart that I can scarcely hold my own. For he is an adversary who never lets up, never tires, and no sooner has one attack ended than new and different ones begin.

Your only help or comfort at such times is to hurry for refuge into the Lord's Prayer and to appeal to God from the heart, "Dear Father, You have commanded me to pray; do not let me fall into this temptation." You will then see the temptation lessening, until it finally admits defeat. On the other hand, if you try to save yourself by your own devices of thought and feeling, you will only make a bad situation worse and give the devil a better opening. For he has the head of a serpent; if he finds a gap through which his head can slip, the whole length of his body wriggles in unchecked. Prayer, however, can oppose him and drive him back.

### The Last Petition

*"But deliver us from evil."*

In the Greek this petition reads, "Deliver us from or protect us against the Evil One, or the Wicked One." It seems that the petition is speaking of the devil as the sum of all evil in order to direct the total weight of our collective prayers against our archenemy. He it is who raises barriers among us against all that we pray for—God's name or glory, God's kingdom and will, our daily bread, a good and cheerful conscience, and the like. We therefore wrap all our petitions into one by saying, "Dear Father, help us get rid of all this trouble entirely."

This short petition is nevertheless also directed against specific evils that emanate from the devil's kingdom and may befall us: poverty, dishonor, death, in short, all the wretched miseries and heartaches of which there are so innumerably many on earth. For, being not only a liar but also a murderer, the devil is perpetually engaged in attempts on our life and vents his rage by causing us accidents and bodily harm whenever possible. He breaks many a neck and deranges many a mind; he drowns some persons, and he hounds many into suicide and other dreadful crimes. Therefore, we have an ongoing task on earth, and that is to pray constantly against

96

this archenemy. For if God did not support us, we would not be safe from this foe for a single hour.

From this you can see that God wants us to pray to Him also concerning everything that threatens our bodily welfare, and He wants us to ask help and to expect help from Him alone. However, He placed this petition after the others for the reason that if we are to be shielded against and freed from all evil, His name must first be hallowed within us, His rule extended over us, and His will done by us. Then He will preserve us from sins and shames and from everything else that might hurt or harm us.

Thus God has briefly pointed to all the trouble that may bedevil us, so that we might never have an excuse not to pray. But what effect our prayer will have depends on our learning also to say "Amen" to it—that is, not to doubt that the prayer is certainly heard and that it will be granted. "Amen" is simply the expression of an unquestioning faith that prayer is not a gamble and that God certainly is not lying when He promises to grant what we pray for. Now, where such faith is absent, there also the prayer is not genuine.

It is therefore a hurtful delusion when people so pray that they dare not wholeheartedly add their "Yes, it shall be so" nor conclude with certainty that God hears their prayer, but instead remain doubtful and say, "How dare I have the audacity to boast that God heard my prayer? After all, I am only a poor sinner," etc. This shows that they are fastening their gaze not on God's promise but on their own works and their own worthiness, thus despising God and calling Him a liar. Therefore they receive nothing, as St. James says (1:6-8): "But let him ask in faith, with no doubting, for he who doubts is like a wave of the sea that is driven and tossed by the wind. For that person must not suppose that a double-minded man, unstable in all his ways, will receive anything from the Lord." See how intensely God desires that we should have the confident certainty that we are not praying in vain and that we should by no means view our prayers with a disparaging eye.

### Fourth Part

BAPTISM

We have now taken care of the three chief parts of Christian teaching. It remains for us to speak of our two sacraments instituted by Christ. Every Christian should at least have some brief general instruction about them—although in the past unfortunately nothing was taught about them—because without the sacraments no one can be a Christian. We shall first take up Baptism, through which we were originally received into the Christian community. In order that it may be easily grasped, we shall deal with it systematically and confine ourselves to what is necessary to know about it. We shall leave it to the learned to show how one must maintain and defend Baptism against heretics and sects.

In the first place, we must above all know well the words on which Baptism is founded and toward which everything that we can say about it is focused, namely the words of the Lord Christ in the last chapter of Matthew, "Go therefore and make disciples of all nations, baptizing them in the name of the Father and of the Son and of the Holy Ghost" (Matthew 28:19). Likewise in the last chapter of Mark, "He who believes and is baptized will be saved; but he who does not believe will be condemned" (Mark 16:16).

You should first of all note that these words stand as God's command and ordinance. Basing yourself on these words, you are not to doubt that Baptism is a divine act, not something devised or invented by man. For as truly as I can affirm that the Ten Commandments, the Creed, and the Lord's Prayer were not spun out of any human being's head, but revealed and given by God Himself, so joyously can I affirm that Baptism is no human trifle, but that it was established by God Himself. Moreover, He earnestly and solemnly commanded that we must be baptized or we shall not be saved. No one is to think that it is an optional matter like putting on a red coat. It is of the greatest importance that we hold Baptism in high esteem as something splendid and glorious. The reason why we are striving and battling so strenuously for this view of Baptism is that the world nowadays is full of sects that loudly proclaim that Baptism is merely an external form and that external forms are useless. Well, be it external as it may, nevertheless here stands God's Word and command that institutes, establishes, and confirms Baptism. And what God institutes and commands cannot be useless; it is altogether priceless and precious, even though it were as insignificant in appearance as a spear of straw. If in the past people were able to imagine it a great thing for the pope to dispense indulgences with his letters and bulls, and to consecrate altars and churches simply by means of his

98

documents and their papal seals, then we certainly should regard Baptism as much more exalted and precious because it was commanded by God. Moreover, Baptism is performed in His name. For that is how the words read, "Go, baptize," not, however, in your name but in God's name.

To be baptized in God's name is to be baptized not by man but by God Himself. Although Baptism is indeed performed by human hands, yet it is truly God's own action. From this everyone can himself easily draw the obvious conclusion that it is a much greater work than that of any human being, even of any saint. For what action of man could be greater than an action of God's?

But here the devil gets busy and tries to blind us with false appearances and deflect us from God's action to our own. For, compared with God's action in Baptism, it makes a much more striking display when a Carthusian monk performs many great difficult works; and we all attach special importance to what we ourselves achieve or perform. But Scripture teaches that even if we heaped together all the works of monks on one pile, no matter how splendidly they might glitter, they would still not be as noble and good as the action of God if He were to pick up a piece of straw. Why is that? Because the person performing the action is better and more noble. Here we must not rate the person according to the work, but the work according to the person from whom the action derives its worth. But lunatic human reason refuses to listen, and because Baptism does not glitter like the works that we do, reason regards it as having no value.

Learn from this to come to a correct understanding and to find the answer to the question, What is Baptism? It is not simple, ordinary water, but water comprehended in God's Word and thus made holy. It is nothing else than a divine water, not because the water in itself is something more special than other water, but because God's Word and commandment are added to it.

Therefore it is sheer wickedness and devilish blasphemy when our new spirit people now mock at Baptism, ignore the Word and ordinance of God, see in it nothing but the water drawn up from a well, and then rattle on, "How can a handful of water help a soul?" Quite right, my friend! If water and Word are separated, who does not know that water is nothing but water? But how dare you thrust your fist into God's ordinance and rip out of it the most priceless jeweled setting with which God has combined it and into which He has set it and from which He does not want it separated! For the central essence of the baptismal water is the Word or commandment of God and the name of God, a treasure that is greater and nobler than heaven and earth.

So then, understand the distinction: Baptism is a vastly different thing than any other water, not because of its natural substance, but because something far more noble is added to it. For God Himself here puts His honor, might, and power on the line. Therefore it is not merely natural water but a divine, heavenly, holy, and blessed water—add whatever terms of praise you will—all because of the Word, which is a heavenly, holy Word that no one could ever praise enough; for this Word contains and transmits all of God's fullness. It is from the Word that Baptism derives its nature as a sacrament, as St. Augustine has taught: *"Accedat verbum ad elementum et fit sacramentum,"* which means, "When the Word is joined to the element or natural substance, the outcome is a sacrament," that is, a holy, divine thing and sign.

Therefore we constantly teach that the sacraments and all external things that God ordained and established are not to be evaluated on the basis of their coarse, outward form, as when we see the outer shell of a nut, but rather as something in which the Word of God is enclosed. We speak about parenthood and civil authority in the same way. If we consider the persons with reference to their noses, eyes, skin and hair, flesh and bone, then they will look no different than Turks and heathen. Someone might come along and say, "Why should I think more of this person than of others?" Yet because of the attached commandment, "You shall honor father and mother," I see quite another person, one clothed and adorned with the majesty and glory of God. The commandment, I say, is the golden chain which that person is wearing around his neck; yes, it is the crown on his head that tells me how and why I should honor this ordinary flesh and blood person.

In the same manner, and much more so, you should honor and highly prize Baptism as something glorious for the sake of the Word, God Himself having honored it both by word and action, besides certifying it with wonders from heaven. Do you imagine that it was a jest when Christ submitted to Baptism and the heavens opened and the Holy Spirit descended visibly and there was nothing but glory and majesty all around?

I therefore urge you once again that these two, Word and water, dare by no means be parted and separated from each other. For when the Word is taken away from it, the water is no different than that with which the maid does her cooking, in which case it might just as well be called a bathhouse washing. But when the Word is present as God ordained it to be, then it is a sacrament and is called Baptism by Christ. This is the first point to be stressed: the nature and dignity of the holy Sacrament of Baptism.

In the second place, since we now know what Baptism is and how we should regard it, we must also learn why and for what purpose it was established, that is, what it is useful for, what it gives to us, and what it creates in us. This cannot be stated better than in the words of Christ quoted above, "He who believes and is baptized will be saved" (Mark 16:16). Stated most simply, the power, effect, benefit, fruit, and purpose of Baptism is to save. No one is baptized for the purpose of making him a prince, but as the words say, that he may "be saved." To become saved is, as we know, nothing else than to be delivered from sins, from death, and from the devil, and to come into Christ's kingdom and live with Him forever.

There you see again what a priceless value is to be attached to Baptism, since in it we obtain such an inexpressibly great treasure. This definitely shows that there is more here than simply ordinary water, for mere water could not have such an effect. What produces this effect is that the Word and (as stated above) the name of God is present in it. Where God's name is, there life and salvation must be present also. For this reason Baptism is rightly called a divine, blessed, fruitful, and gracious water. For it receives its power through the Word, the power to be a "washing of regeneration," as Paul calls it in Titus 3:5.

But our know-it-alls, the new spirit people, claim that faith alone saves and that human works and outward forms contribute nothing to this. We answer: It is of course true that nothing in us does it except faith, as we shall hear later. But these blind leaders of the blind refuse to see that faith must have something in which it believes, that is, something it clings to, something on which to plant its feet and into which to sink its roots. Thus faith clings to the water and believes Baptism to be something in which there is pure salvation and life, not through the water, as I have emphasized often enough, but because God's name is joined to it. Now, if I believe this, what else am I doing than believing in God as the One who has taken His Word and planted it into this external thing that He hands us in order that we might get a grip on the treasure He put into it?

Now, it is absurd for these people to separate faith from the thing to which it adheres and to which it is bound, arguing that that thing is something external. Certainly, it should and must be external so that the senses can perceive and grasp it and it thus can be brought into the heart. Indeed, the entire Gospel is an external proclamation in language form. In fact, whatever God does and effects in us, He wants to do through such external arrangements. Wherever God speaks—yes, to whatever purpose or through whatever means He speaks—that is where faith should fix its gaze, that is the thing that faith should hold on to. Now, here we have the words, "He who believes and is baptized will be saved." To what do they refer but to Baptism, that is, the water embraced in God's ordinance? It follows from this that whoever rejects Baptism rejects God's Word, faith, and the Christ who directs us to Baptism and binds us to it.

In the third place, having understood the great benefit and power of Baptism, let us take note who the persons are who receive the benefits that Baptism offers. This, too, is most precisely and clearly expressed in these same words, "He who believes and is baptized will be saved." That is to say, it is faith alone that makes a person worthy to receive the divine, healing water to his benefit. Since all the blessings are offered and promised in the words that accompany the water, therefore they cannot be received otherwise than by wholeheartedly believing in them. Without faith Baptism becomes useless, although in itself it is a divine, infinitely wonderful treasure. So this single phrase "he who believes" is so strong that it can drive out and shut the gates against all the works a man might do with the notion of earning and achieving his salvation through them. For here it is firmly settled that anything that is not faith accomplishes nothing toward salvation and receives nothing whatever.

But suppose they say, as they usually do, "Since Baptism is in itself a work and you say that works contribute nothing to salvation, where then does faith come in?" To that you should answer: It is true, our works of course contribute nothing to salvation, but Baptism is not our work but God's (for, as stated, you must distinguish Christ's Baptism most sharply from a bathhouse washing). God's works, however, are health-giving and necessary for our salvation, and they do not exclude but demand faith, for without faith the works of God could not be grasped and held. It is not by your mere act of letting water be poured over you that you grasp and keep hold of the blessings so that they will benefit you. On the contrary, the blessings conveyed in Baptism benefit you when you let yourself be baptized in the name of God on the basis of His command and ordinance in order to receive the salvation God has promised. Now, this the hand or the body cannot do; it is something that the heart must believe.

Thus you can clearly see that Baptism is not a work that we do, but a treasure that God gives us and that our faith grasps, even as the Lord Christ on the cross is not a human work but a treasure contained in the Word, offered to us by the Word, and received by faith in the Word. Therefore, those do us an injustice who loudly protest that in our preaching we oppose faith. The fact is, we are constantly insisting on faith as being so necessary that without it nothing can be received, nothing enjoyed.

We have thus considered the three points about this sacrament that we must know, especially—and this alone would be enough—that it is God's ordinance and that it is to be held in highest esteem even though it is a completely external action. In a similar way, "You shall honor your father and mother" refers only to human flesh and blood, yet here we are to regard not the mere physical selves but God's commandment in which they are comprehended and because of which they are called father and mother. So also, even if we had no more than these words, "Go and baptize," etc., we would nevertheless have to accept Baptism as God's ordinance and practice it. Here, however, we have not only the commandment and directive but also the promise. Thus Baptism is much more glorious than what God has otherwise commanded and ordained without such a promise. In short, Baptism is so full of comfort and grace that heaven and earth cannot fathom it. It requires special insight to believe this; for, there being no deficiency in the treasure, the deficiency lies in a person's failure to grasp the treasure and hold it in a firm grip.

Every Christian consequently has enough to learn and to practice all his life in regard to Baptism. For he will always have enough to do in order steadfastly to believe what

Baptism assures and offers to him: victory over the devil and over death, forgiveness of sins, God's grace, the fullness of Christ, and the Holy Spirit with His gifts. In short, the blessings of Baptism are so infinitely great that if someone who is naturally timid thinks about them, he might well doubt whether it could all be true. Just consider this, that if there were some physician who could with his skill keep people from dying, or after they have died could give them endless life, what a blizzard and deluge of money the world would snow and rain upon him! It would be impossible to get to him through the crowds of the affluent. Now here in Baptism there is brought free of charge to everyone's door the very sort of priceless medicine that swallows up death and saves the lives of all people.

The way to regard and use Baptism rightly is to draw strength and comfort from it when our sins or consciences trouble us. We then must say, "See here, I am baptized. And since I am baptized, I have the assurance that I shall be saved in soul and body and have eternal life." This is why these two things are done in Baptism: Water is poured on the body, which can sense no more than the water, and at the same time the Word is spoken for the soul to take hold of.

Now, since water and Word together constitute one Baptism, body and soul together will be saved and live forever, the soul through the Word in which it believes, the body because it is united with the soul and takes the Baptism in the only way it can. There is no greater jewel than Baptism for adorning our body and soul, for through it we become perfectly holy and are completely saved, something that otherwise no manner of life and no effort on earth can attain.

Let this be enough for the present purpose concerning the nature, benefits, and use of Baptism.

### Infant Baptism

At this point a question arises that the devil uses to confuse the world through his sects, the question of infant Baptism. Can also children believe, and may they rightfully be baptized? To this we answer briefly: Let simple and unlearned folk put the question out of their minds and let the learned discuss it.

But if you must answer the question, then answer as follows: The fact that infant Baptism pleases Christ is amply proved by His own activity, that is to say that the Lord sanctified and gave the Holy Spirit to many who were baptized as infants. And in our day still there is many a one from whose doctrine and life one perceives that he has the Holy Spirit. The Spirit is given also to us by the grace of God, so that we are able to interpret the Scriptures and to know Christ, which could not happen without Him. Now, if it were so that God does not accept infant Baptism as valid, then he would not give the Holy Spirit, not even a bit of Him, to anyone baptized in infancy. In short, in all the long time from the past down to the present, there could not have been Christians on earth if infant Baptism were not valid. Since God has confirmed infant Baptism by giving His Holy Spirit, as is perfectly recognizable in such church fathers as St. Bernard, Gerson, John Hus, and others who were baptized in infancy, and since the Holy Christian church will continue to the end of the world, our opponents must acknowledge that infant Baptism is pleasing to God. For he can never go against Himself, foster lies and evils, or give His grace and Spirit for such purposes. This is about the best and strongest proof for simple and unlearned persons. For this article of the faith, "I believe in one holy Christian church, the communion of saints; etc.," no one can take from us, no one can overthrow.

Furthermore, our prime concern here is not whether or not the baptized person believes; for if he does not believe, his Baptism itself does not on that account become invalid. Everything depends instead on God's Word and promise. This point is perhaps a little subtle, but it is based on what I said previously, that Baptism is nothing else than water and God's Word joined in and with each other; this means that when the Word comes together with the water, then the Baptism is valid even if faith is lacking in the person being baptized. For my faith does not make Baptism what it is; rather, faith accepts what Baptism is. So Baptism does not become invalid even if it is wrongly taken or used, for it is bound not to our faith but to the Word.

For even though this very day a Jew were to come with deceitfulness and evil intent and we in good faith baptized him, we would nevertheless have to affirm that the Baptism was valid. For the water would be there together with the Word, even though the man did not receive it as he should have done. Here the situation is the same as for those who partake unworthily of the Lord's Supper: they receive the true sacrament even though they do not believe.

So you see that the objections of the sectarians are worth nothing. As we said, even if infants did not believe (which, however, is not the case, as we have proved), yet their Baptism would be valid, and no one should baptize them again. It is here as with the Lord's Supper, which is not nullified even for a person who might have received it with evil intent; he would not, in view of his misuse of it, be allowed to take it again in the same worship hour, as if he had not really received the Sacrament in the first place. That would be blaspheming and desecrating the Sacrament in the worst possible way. How could we dare to suppose that the Word and ordinance of God would become wrong and invalid because of our wrong use of it?

I therefore say this: If you did not believe before this, then believe now and confess, "My Baptism was indeed a right Baptism, but, sad to say, I did not receive it rightly." Even I myself, and all who come for Baptism, must say before God, "I come here in my faith and also in the faith of others; nevertheless, I cannot build on the fact that I have faith or that many people of faith are praying for me. Rather, I build on this, that it is Your word and command." Similarly, I go to the Sacrament of the Lord's Table, not on the basis of the fact that I believe, but on the basis of the Word of Christ. The question whether I am strong or weak in the faith I leave in God's hands. But this I know, that He tells me to go, eat and drink, etc., and that He there will give me His body and His blood. He does not lie about this or deceive me.

We do the same kind of thing also in infant Baptism. We carry the child to the font with the purpose and the hope that he may believe, and we pray that God would give him faith; but it is not on the strength of that purpose, that hope, or that expected creation of faith in the child that we baptize the child, but simply because God has commanded it. Why? Because we know that God does not lie. I, my neighbor, in short, all men may err and deceive, but the Word of God cannot err.

It is only rash and blockheaded persons who draw the conclusion that where there is no true faith, there can be no true Baptism. This is like arguing that if I have no faith in Christ, then Christ is nothing, or that if I am disobedient, then father, mother, and superiors are nothing. When someone does not do the thing he ought to do, is it a valid conclusion to say that the thing itself does not exist or is worthless? My friend, turn the argument the other way around and conclude: Precisely because the Baptism was in a certain instance received wrongfully, therefore it is something that does exist and does have value. For if Baptism were not right in and of itself, we could not misuse it or sin against it. The saying is, *"Abusus non tollit, sed confirmat substantiam,"* that is, "Abuse does not destroy the substance, but rather demonstrates its existence." For gold remains none the less gold though a harlot wears it in sin and shame.

Let it stand as firmly settled, then, that Baptism at all times remains valid and retains its full character, even if only one person had been baptized and if, on top of this, he did not have the true faith. For the ordinance and Word of God refuses to let itself be changed or altered by man. But the fanatics are so blinded that they do not see God's Word and command. They regard Baptism as being no more than the water in the stream or in the bucket; as for government officials, these they see only as ordinary persons. Because they are thus blind to both faith and obedience, therefore they also imagine the ordinances to be invalid that God established as objects of faith and obedience. Here lurks a sneaking insurrectionist devil who would enjoy snatching the crown from the rulers to have it trampled under foot and would in addition like to pervert and ruin for us all the works and ordinances of God. We must therefore be vigilant and well armed and not allow ourselves to be shifted or turned aside from the Word so as to take Baptism to be merely an empty sign, as the fanatics dream it is.

Lastly, we must also know what Baptism signifies and why God ordained precisely this outward sign and external observance for that sacrament by which we are first received into the Christian church. This act or rite consists in dipping us into water, which covers us, and then drawing us out of the water again. These two parts of the rite, the dipping beneath the water and the emerging again, point to Baptism's power and effect, which are simply the slaying of the old Adam and the resurrection of the new man. Both of these actions are to keep happening in us throughout our life on earth. A Christian life is thus nothing else than an ongoing daily Baptism, once begun and always continuing. We must keep at it without interruption, always sweeping out what relates to the old Adam and letting that which belongs to the new man flourish. But what is the old man? He is what is born in us by inheritance from Adam; he is wrathful, hateful, envious, impure, miserly, lazy, proud, yes, unbelieving, full of vices, having no good in him by nature. Now, when we come into Christ's kingdom, these pollutions should daily diminish, so that the longer we live the more gentle, patient, and good-tempered we become, and the more we break with greed, hate, envy, and pride.

This is the right use of Baptism among Christians, which use is signified by the baptizing with water. Where this amendment of life is not in progress and the old man is instead given free rein so that he keeps getting stronger, there Baptism is not being used properly but is being undermined. Those who live outside of Christ cannot but become worse every day, as the proverb correctly says, "The longer evil remains unchecked, the worse it becomes." If someone was proud and greedy a year ago, he will today be much greedier and prouder. From his youth up vice grows in him and never stops growing. A young child, who has no particular vice, becomes disorderly and unchaste as he grows. When he comes to full manhood, the real vices take hold more and more.

The old man therefore continues unhindered along the course set by his nature if he is not checked and suppressed through the power of Baptism. On the other hand, when we become Christians, the old man sinks day by day until he finally goes under. This is truly an immersion into Baptism and a daily reemergence. So the outward rite is designed not only to do its mighty work but also to signify something. Where faith is alive together with its fruits, there Baptism is not an empty symbol but is effectively at work. But where faith is absent, there Baptism remains a mere barren sign.

Here you see that Baptism, both in what its power can do and in what it signifies, includes also the third sacrament, formerly called Penance, which is essentially the same as Baptism. For what is repentance but a determined attack on the old man and an entry into a new life? If you, therefore, live in repentance, you are progressing in your Baptism, which not only heralds the new life but also creates, begins, and carries it forward. For in Baptism we are given the grace, the Spirit, and the power to put down the old man, so that the new man may come forth and grow to maturity.

Thus Baptism remains in force forever, and although a person falls out of his Baptism into sin, yet we always have an access back into it, so that we may again and again throw the old man and pin him down. But water need not be poured over us again. For even if we let ourselves be immersed in water a hundred times, it would still be no more than one Baptism; but the effectiveness and significance of Baptism are ongoing and never cease. Thus repentance is nothing else than a return to Baptism, a reentry into Baptism, in order to resume and carry forward what was begun earlier but then discontinued.

I say this in order that we may not adopt the opinion that long prevailed among us, that our Baptism is past and can never be used after we again have fallen into sin. The reason for a notion of this sort is that one looks upon Baptism in its aspect of a one-time action. Indeed, the idea goes back to St. Jerome, who wrote, "Repentance is the second plank on which we must swim ashore after the sinking of the ship" in which we embarked and sailed forth when we entered the Christian church at Baptism. This view deprives us of the use of Baptism, so that it can no longer benefit us. Jerome's statement is not correct, for the ship, Baptism, cannot be shipwrecked because, as we said, it is God's ordinance and not something of ours. It can happen, however, that we slip and fall out of the ship. But when this happens and someone does fall out, he should at once swim for the ship again and cling to it until he can climb back on deck and sail forward as he had earlier begun to do.

Thus we see how splendid a thing Baptism is. It snatches us out of the devil's jaws, makes God our own, defeats and puts away sin, daily strengthens the new man in us, keeps functioning, and remains with us until we leave our present troubles to enter glory everlasting.

Everyone should therefore look upon his Baptism as his everyday wear, to be worn constantly. He should at all times be found in faith and surrounded by its fruits. He should every day suppress the old man and grow toward maturity in the new man. For if we want to be Christians, we must carry on in the work that makes us Christians. But if someone falls away from it, let him come back to it again. For just as Christ, the throne of divine mercy, does not withdraw from us nor prevent us from coming back again to Him, though we sin, so also all His treasures and gifts remain. As we once obtained forgiveness of sins in Baptism, so that forgiveness continues for us as long as we live, that is to say, for as long as we have the old Adam hanging about our necks.

## Fifth Part

## THE SACRAMENT OF THE ALTAR

Having treated Holy Baptism under a threefold division, we must likewise speak of the second sacrament under three headings, stating what it is, what its benefits are, and who should receive it. The discussion of these points will be based on the words by which Christ instituted it. Everyone who wishes to be a Christian and go to this sacrament should be familiar with these words. For we do not intend to grant admission to the Sacrament and distribute it to those who do not know what they are looking for or why they are coming. The words are these:

*"Our Lord Jesus Christ, on the night when He was betrayed, took bread, gave thanks, broke it, and gave it to His disciples and said, 'Take, eat; this is My body, which is given for you. Do this in remembrance of Me.' "*

*"In the same way also He took the cup, after supper, gave thanks, and gave it to them, saying, 'This cup is the new testament in My blood, which is poured out for you for the forgiveness of sins. Do this, as often as you drink it, in remembrance of Me.' "*

We do not at this time wish to tangle and fight with those who defame and desecrate this sacrament, but we shall first learn, as we did in the case of Baptism, what the source of its power is, namely God's Word and ordinance or command, which is the chief thing. For the Lord's Supper was not invented or introduced by any man. It was Christ who instituted it without following anyone else's thinking or advice. As a result, this blessed sacrament retains its complete wholeness and integrity despite our misuse or mishandling of it. It is with the Sacrament as with the Ten Commandments, the Lord's Prayer, and the Creed: even if we never keep the Ten Commandments, pray the Lord's Prayer, or believe the Creed, these all retain their character and majesty in spite of us. Do you imagine that God is so dependent on our conduct and faith that He will let them cause Him to make shifts and changes in His ordinance? Surely, in worldly matters everything remains as God created and ordered it, regardless of how we use and handle it. We must keep insisting upon this, for here is an argument with which thoroughly to refute the nonsense of the rabble-rousing spirits who think of the sacraments as detached from

110

God's Word and as something we do rather than as something God does.

Now, what is the Sacrament of the Altar? Answer: It is the true body and blood of the Lord Christ in and under the bread and wine, which Christ's Word commands us to eat and to drink. We said that Baptism is not mere water; just so we say here that this sacrament is bread and wine, but not mere bread and wine such as is otherwise served at table. Rather, it is bread and wine comprehended in God's Word and connected with it.

It is, I affirm, the Word that makes this sacrament what it is and distinguishes it from ordinary bread and wine; the Word causes it to be Christ's body and blood, as it is rightly to be called. For as the saying goes, *"Accedat verbum ad elementum et fit sacramentum,"* "When the Word is joined to the external element, it becomes a sacrament." This saying of St. Augustine's is so accurately to the point, so well put, that he can hardly have made any better statement. The Word must make the element a sacrament, otherwise it remains mere element. The Word and ordinance establishing this sacrament is not that of a prince or emperor, but that of the divine Majesty, at whose feet all the world should kneel to give their Yes to what He says, affirming that it is exactly so, and accepting it with all reverence, fear, and humility.

With the Word you can strengthen your conscience and say, "Though a hundred thousand devils, plus all the fanatics, come rushing up to question how bread and wine can be Christ's body and blood, still I know that all the fanatic spirits and all the scholars heaped together cannot match the wisdom that the divine Majesty has in His little finger. Here stands Christ with the Word, 'Take, eat; this is My body.' 'Drink of it, all of you, this is the new covenant in My blood,' etc. That is where we shall take our stand and watch the futile attempts of those who would play the schoolmaster with God and try to alter what He has spoken. It is true, of course, that if you take away the Word from the Sacrament and look at the elements apart from the Word, you will have nothing but ordinary bread and wine. But if the words of Christ remain connected with the elements, as they should, as they must, then the true body and the true blood of Christ are present, as the words say. For as it was spoken by Christ's own lips, so it is; He cannot lie or deceive."

Having His Word, it is easy to answer all sorts of

questions that are now troubling people—for example, whether even a wicked priest can administer the Sacrament, and other questions like that. Our firm conclusion is: even though a scoundrel receives the Sacrament or administers it, it is the true Sacrament, that is, Christ's body and blood, exactly the same as when someone uses it in the most worthy manner possible. For the validity of the Lord's Supper is not based on man's holiness, but on God's Word. And just as no saint on earth, yes, no angel in heaven can turn bread and wine into Christ's body and blood, so also no one can change or alter the Sacrament even when he misuses it. The Word by which it was constituted and established as a Sacrament does not become false on account of an individual's unworthiness or unbelief. Christ does not say, "If you believe or are worthy, then you receive My body and blood," but, "Take, eat and drink, this is My body and blood." And he also says, "Do this," namely, "Do this that I now do, institute, and give to you, and tell you to take." This is as much as to say, "Regardless of whether you are unworthy or worthy, you here have Christ's body and blood through the power of these words that are joined with the bread and wine." Take note of these words and remember them well. For these words are the basis of our entire cause; they are its protection and defense against all errors and deceptions that ever arose or that may still arise.

Thus we have briefly dealt with the first point, concerning the essence of this sacrament. We come now to the power and the benefit of the Sacrament, the real purpose for which it was instituted. It is most necessary to grasp what its power and its benefit are in order to know what to look for and what to get out of the Sacrament. This is clearly evident from the words just quoted: "This is My body and blood given and poured out *for you* for the forgiveness of sins." In other words, we go to the Sacrament because there we receive a great treasure through which and in which we obtain the forgiveness of sins. Why is that? Because there are the words, and it is they that give us this forgiveness. This is why Christ bids me to eat and to drink: He wants the Sacrament to be mine and to be a blessing to me as a sure pledge and sign of the treasure—yes, to be the very treasure itself which is my security against sin, death, and all evils.

Therefore it is fitting to call it the food of the soul that nourishes and strengthens the new man. It is of course through Baptism that we are first born anew. But it must be said here, as before, that human flesh and blood still retain their old skin. We often grow faint and weary and sometimes even stumble as the devil and the world confront us with their many obstacles and temptations. That is why the Lord's Supper is given us for daily food and sustenance to refresh and strengthen us, so that our faith may not become weary in battle but go from strength to strength. For the new life should be a constant forward progress. It must, meanwhile, suffer much opposition. The devil is a furious adversary; when he sees that we resist him and are on the offensive against our old self, and when he realizes that he cannot overrun us by force, he slithers and sneaks in from every side, testing out all his tricks on us, and he does not give up until he has worn us down to the point where we either discard faith or surrender hand and foot to apathy or impatience. It is for such times when we are disheartened and under heavy pressure that this comfort of the Lord's Supper is given. There we are to find refreshment and renew our strength.

But here again the clever spirits, contorted with their great learning and wisdom, come blustering and bellowing, "How can bread and wine forgive sin and strengthen faith?" Yet they know well enough that we do not attribute this power to the bread and the wine—in itself bread is but bread—but to the bread and wine that are Christ's body and blood and with which the words are connected. These alone, we repeat, are the treasure through which the forgiveness was won for us. The treasure is communicated to us in no other way than through the words "given and shed for you." There you have the truth both that this is Christ's body and blood and that these are yours, a treasure and a gift that belongs to you. Christ's body can never be an unfruitful, vain thing that accomplishes nothing and benfits no one. Yet, however great the treasure may be in itself, it must be caught up by the Word and handed to us through the Word; otherwise we could never know about it or seek it.

Therefore it is absurd for them to say that one cannot have forgiveness of sins in the Sacrament because the body and blood of Christ were given and shed for us elsewhere than in the Lord's Supper. For although the work was accomplished and forgiveness of sins acquired for us on the cross, yet the only way it can come to us is through the Word. How could we know what it was that happened or what is to be given to us if it were not for the proclamation, the oral Word? Where do people learn about forgiveness or how can they lay hold on it and appropriate it, unless they hold and believe the Scriptures and the Gospel? Now, the whole of the Gospel and this article of the Creed, "I believe in the holy Christian church, the forgiveness of sins, etc.," are incorporated in the Sacrament and there offered to us through the Word. Why, then, should we let such a treasure be torn out of the Sacrament? Our opponents must agree after all that here in the Sacrament is the very message we hear everywhere in the Gospel. As little as they dare say that the whole Gospel or Word of God outside of the Sacrament is valueless, so little can they say that the words in the Sacrament are valueless.

Up to this point we have been considering the Sacrament itself both in regard to its essence and in regard to its effect and blessing. It remains for us to point out who are the recipients of such power and blessing. Briefly stated, as was done earlier in connection with Baptism and often elsewhere, the recipients of the Sacrament's effect and blessing are those who believe what the words say and what they offer. For the words are not spoken to a stone or a block of wood but to the hearers to whom Christ says, "Take and eat," etc. And since what He offers and promises is the forgiveness of sins, this gift can be taken in no other way than by faith in the Word. He Himself calls for such faith in the Word when He says, "given FOR YOU" and "shed FOR YOU," as if to say, "I give this to you and tell you to eat and drink in order that you may take it as your own and enjoy it." Whoever takes these words as addressed to him and believes that they are true, he has what the words declare. But whoever does not believe has nothing because he lets this healing grace and blessing be offered to him in vain and refuses to enjoy it. The treasure is opened wide and placed at everyone's door, yes, on everyone's table. But it remains for you to take it, confidently believing that everything is exactly as the words say.

This, then, is the complete preparation Christians need in order to receive this sacrament worthily. Since the treasure is presented entirely in words, it can be seized and appropriated only by the heart that trusts the words. A gift of this kind, an eternal treasure such as this, cannot be taken with the hand. Fasting, prayer, and the like, may well be used by way of outward preparation and elementary discipline, so that one's body may behave with proper reverence toward the body and blood of Christ. But the body cannot grasp or appropriate the benefit that is given in the Sacrament. This can only be done by the faith in a heart that recognizes what the treasure is and desires to have it.

Let this be enough instruction about the essentials of this sacrament. What remains to be said on this score belongs to another occasion.

Now that we have a correct understanding and doctrine of the Sacrament, it may be well to conclude with an admonition and encouragement not to pass up so great a treasure administered and distributed daily among Christians. In other words, let those who profess to be Christians prepare to receive this blessed sacrament often. For it is plain to see that of late people are taking a listless, lazy attitude toward it. A great mass of people, now that the pope's nonsense has been discarded and we are free from his control and authority, go for maybe one, two, three, or more years without receiving the Sacrament. It is as if they were such strong Christians that they do not need it. Some let themselves be deterred and kept away because we taught that no one should go to the Lord's Supper unless drawn by a feeling of hunger and thirst for it. Some others pretend that the Sacrament is optional and not a necessity, and that it is enough that they believe other parts of the Christian faith. Thus the majority become quite loutish and finally scorn both the Sacrament and the Word of God.

It is of course true what we said, that nobody should ever be driven or forced to attend the Lord's Supper, lest a new slaughter of souls begin. We must nevertheless understand that people who absent themselves and abstain for such long periods of time from the Sacrament are not to be taken for Christians. For Christ did not institute it to be treated as a spectator drama, but has commanded His Christians to eat and to drink, and to remember Him as they do so.

True Christians who prize and cherish the Sacrament should indeed motivate and urge themselves to fill the Communion tables. Yet we shall here give a little attention to this point, so that the common people and the weak, who also would like to be Christians, may be stimulated to think about the reason and the need for receiving the Sacrament. In other matters relating to faith, love, and patience, it is not enough simply to teach and instruct; there must also be constant admonition. So here, too, it is necesary to keep on preaching, so that people do not become indifferent to or tired of the Sacrament. For we are well aware that the devil constantly opposes this and every other Christian practice, herding and driving as many as he can away from it.

In the first place, we have for our text the unambiguous words of Christ, "THIS DO in remembrance of Me." By these words the directive and command is issued to us who wish to be Christians that we are to partake of the Sacrament. Anyone who wishes to be counted among the disciples to whom these words are addressed, let him faithfully hold to the Sacrament. Not from compulsion, not under human coercion, but to obey Christ the Lord and please Him. You may perhaps say, "But there are these additional words, 'as often as you do it'; therefore Christ is compelling no one, but is leaving it up to our own free choice." We answer: True enough, but that is not the same as saying one need not partake at all. In fact, by His very words "as often as you do it" He is implying that we should partake often. The reason He adds these words is that He wants the Sacrament to be free in the sense of not being bound to a set time as was the Jewish Passover, which the Jews had to eat once every year, specifically on the 14th day of the first full moon, without deviating even by a single day. It is as if Christ thereby wished to say, "I am instituting a Passover or Supper for you, which you are to enjoy not just on this one evening of the year but often wherever and whenever you wish, as the individual opportunity or need arises. It is not to be tied to any particular time or place." However, the pope later turned this directive around and again made a Jewish feast out of the Lord's Supper.

You see, then, that we are not granted freedom to scorn the Sacrament. I call it scorning the Sacrament when a person, though there is nothing to hinder his attendance, lets a long time pass without ever desiring the Lord's Supper. If you want the liberty to do that, then you may as well take the further liberty of not being a Christian so that you need not believe or pray; for the one is just as much a commandment of Christ as the other. But if you want to be a Christian, then you must find times to satisfy and obey this commandment. For it should keep you motivated to look inward and to say to yourself, "Look here, what kind of Christian am I anyway? If I really were one, then surely I would have at least some little desire to do what my Lord commanded me to do."

Since our attitude is so negative toward the Sacrament, we surely have an indication what kind of Christians we were under the papacy, attending the Sacrament merely from compulsion and the fear of human commands, without joy and without love and even without any regard for the commandment of Christ. We, however, force or compel no one, nor should anyone partake of the Lord's Supper just to serve or please us. But what should draw and even impel you to come is that Christ wishes it and that it will please Him. You should never again let yourself be forced by men into the faith or into any good work. All that we are doing is to urge you to do what you ought to do, not for our sake but for your own. Your Lord invites and encourages you; if you despise that, then you yourself must answer for it.

The first point we are making, especially for the benefit of the cold and indifferent, is that they should come to their senses and wake up. It is certain, as I myself experienced and as everyone else will find to be true in his own case, that if a person stays away from the Lord's Supper day after day he will become more and more callous and cold to it and finally reject it altogether. The alternative is to keep examining our hearts and consciences and to act like persons who would really like to be on right terms with God. The more we do this, the more our hearts will be warmed and kindled and will avoid freezing up completely.

But suppose you say, "What if I feel unfit?" Answer. I am tempted the same way, which is a carry-over from our former situation under the pope. There we tortured ourselves with efforts to become so totally pure that God might not find the least flaw in us; as a result we all became so timid that we easily took fright and would say, "O how unfit I am." At that point human nature and reason begin to measure our unworthiness against the greatness of the Sacrament's priceless treasure, in comparison with which our unrighteousness seems like a smoke-darkened lantern in the brightness of the sun, or like junk in comparison with jewelry. Nature and reason, seeing this contrast, keep people from going to the Sacrament until they feel more prepared. But one week becomes another, and one half-year leads to the next. If you insist on weighing how good and pure you are and if you wait until you feel no stings of conscience, you will never approach the Lord's Table.

We must therefore make a distinction between people. The rude and disorderly are to be told to stay away, for they are not fit to receive the forgiveness of sins because they do not desire it and do not want to lead a good life. As for the rest who are not such coarse and loose-living people and would like to live right, they should not stay away even if they are spiritually weak and sickly. As St. Hilary put it, "Unless a person has committed the sort of sin by which he forfeits Christianity and can be expelled from the congregation, he should not exclude himself from the Sacrament" lest he deprive himself of life. For no one will ever reach a level where he no longer has the many common defects in his blood and flesh.

People who are troubled about this should learn that the highest wisdom is the realization that this sacrament does not depend on our worthiness. We do not come to be baptized because we are worthy and holy, nor do we come to confession because we are pure and without sin. On the contrary, we come as poor, miserable humans precisely because we are unworthy, unless there be someone who desires no grace and absolution nor intends to amend his life.

But he who really wants grace and consolation should push himself into going and should let no one make him shy away. What he should say is, "I would really like to be worthy, but I come not on the basis of any worthiness in me but on account of Your Word, because You commanded it, and, no matter what the state of my worthiness, I want to be a follower of Yours." This is a difficult thing to say and do, for there is always this obstacle and hindrance, that we focus more on our own selves than on the words from the lips of Christ. For human nature likes to act only when it feels sure that it can stand solidly on its own merits; otherwise it won't budge. Let this be enough about the first point.

Second, in addition to the commandment there is also a promise, referred to above, that should most powerfully beckon and compel us. Here, gracious and lovely, stand the words, "This is My body, given FOR YOU," "This is My blood, shed FOR YOU for the forgiveness of sins." These words, as I have said, are not addressed to wood or stone, but to me and to you; otherwise Christ might just as well have remained silent and instituted no sacrament. Therefore think yourself into, place yourself personally into this "you," in order that Christ may not speak to you in vain.

In the Lord's Supper He offers to every one of us the treasure He brought from heaven, a treasure to which He invites us most winsomely also in other passages, as when He says in Matthew 11:28, "Come to Me, all who labor and are heavy-laden, and I will give you rest." How truly and tenderly He summons and encourages us for our own highest and greatest good. Therefore it is surely a sin and a shame that we take such a reluctant attitude toward the Sacrament, neglecting it for such long periods that we become quite cold and hard and lose our delight in it and our love for it. Never regard the Sacrament as something harmful from which to flee, but rather as purely wholesome and soothing therapy that is helpful and life-giving both for the soul and for the body. For if the soul is healed, the body is helped as well. How, then, is it that we act as if the Sacrament were a poison and eating it would kill us?

It is true, of course, that those who despise it and live unchristian lives receive it to their harm and condemnation. Nothing can be good or wholesome for such people, just as when a sick person willfully eats and drinks what the doctor has forbidden. But those who feel their weakness, really want to be rid of it, and desire a remedy should regard and use the Sacrament as a priceless antidote against the poison that they carry in them. For here in the Sacrament you receive from the lips of Christ forgiveness of sins, and His forgiveness contains and brings with it God's grace, God's Spirit, all the gifts of the Spirit, and His protection shielding and sheltering you against death, the devil, and all evil.

Thus from God's side there comes to you both the command and the promise of your Lord Christ to move you to receive the Sacrament often. That which should impel you from your side is your own need, that is, your personal problems hanging about your neck. These are the very reason for Christ's command, encouragement, and promise. He Himself says in Matthew 9:12: "Those who are well have no need of a physician, but those who are sick," that is, those who labor and are heavy laden with sin, fear of death, and the temptations of the flesh and the devil. If you are heavy laden and feel your weakness, go joyfully to the Lord's Table and let it refresh, comfort, and strengthen you. If you wait until your burden disappears and you are pure and worthy of the Sacrament, then you will have to stay away forever; for in that event the Lord's verdict will be, "Since you are so pure and good, you do not need Me, nor I you." Actually only those are unworthy who do not feel their sicknesses and will not admit to being sinners.

But suppose you say, "What shall I do if I do not feel this need nor experience hunger and thirst for the Sacrament?" Answer: To those of you whose state of mind is such that you do not feel your need, I can give no better counsel than to tell you to pinch yourselves and see if you still are flesh and blood. If you find that you are, then for your own good, turn to St. Paul's Epistle to the Galatians (5:19, 20) and hear of what sort are the fruits of the flesh: "The works of the flesh are plain: immorality, impurity, licentiousness, idolatry, sorcery, enmity, strife, jealousy, anger, selfishness, dissension, party spirit, envy, drunkenness, carousing, and the like."

So, if you cannot feel your need, at least believe the Scripture. Scripture will not lie to you. It knows you better than you do yourself. Yes, Saint Paul also concludes in Romans 7:18: "I know that nothing good dwells within me, that is, in my flesh." If Saint Paul can say that about his flesh, let us not make ourselves out to be any better or holier than he. But the fact that we do not feel our sinfulness shows that our condition is much worse than his. For it is a sign that our flesh is leprous and does not feel anything even though the disease is raging in us and eating our life away. If sin has deadened you so completely, you better believe the Scripture as it pronounces God's verdict against you. In short, the less you feel your sins and flaws, the more reason you have to go to the Sacrament to seek a remedy.

In the second place, look around you to see if you are still in the world. Or if you do not know whether you are, then ask your neighbor. And if you find, as you will, that you are indeed still in the world, do not think that there will be any lack of sins and troubles. Just begin acting as if you want to become a good person and stay with the Gospel, and then see if people will not turn against you, do you harm, injustice, and violence, thus giving you occasion for sin and wrongdoing. If you have not experienced this, learn it from Scripture, which everywhere testifies that this is what the world is like.

You will certainly also, in addition to the flesh and the world, have the devil about you. Him you will not completely tread under foot, because not even our Lord Christ could entirely avoid His temptations. Now, what is the devil? Nothing else than what the Scripture calls him, a liar and a murderer. He is a liar who seduces the heart away from God's Word and blinds it, so that you become insensitive to your need and unable to come to Christ. He is a murderer who begrudges you every hour of your life. If you could see how many of his knives, spears, and arrows are aimed at you every moment, you would be glad to come to the Sacrament as often as you can. The one reason why we go about so heedlessly in our false sense of security is that we do not admit or believe that we are living in the flesh, in the world, and in the devil's domain.

Here, therefore, is something for you to try; practice it well: Look down deep into yourself; look round about you a little; and simply hold to what Scripture says about it all. If after doing this you still feel no need of the Sacrament, then you have all the more reason to lay your trouble before both God and your brother. Seek the counsel of others, and let them pray for you, and be sure not to give up until the rocky crust of your heart is broken. The trouble you are in will then be laid open to view, and you will become aware that you have sunk twice as low as any other poor sinner and are in much greater need than he of the Sacrament in order to overcome the misery which unfortunately you did not see. Be sure to do this. God may give you grace to become more sensitive to your need and hungrier for the Sacrament. You should do this especially because in his attempt to capture and ruin you, soul and body, the devil is pressuring and pursuing you so hard that you cannot be safe from him for a single hour. How much he would like to bring you into sudden misery and trouble when you least expect it!

Let this serve as an exhortation not only for us older grown-ups but also for the young people, who are to be brought up in Christian doctrine and its right understanding. It might help to make it easier to instill the Ten Commandments, the Creed, and the Lord's Prayer into the young, so that they would gladly and genuinely accept them and put them early into habitual use. For we are really at the point where we can do no more with older people in order to assure the perpetuation of these and similar teachings. All we can expect to do is to train the people who are to come after us and step into our office and work, so that in their turn they will bring up their children well. In this way God's Word and the Christian church will be preserved. Therefore let every head of a family remember that God's injunction and command makes him responsible to teach his children, or to have them taught, what they ought to know. Having been baptized and taken up into the Christian church, the young people should also enjoy this fellowship of the Sacrament, so that they may become useful and of service to us. For surely they are all to help us to live lives of faith, love, and prayer, and to fight against the devil.

Here now follows an exhortation to confession.

121

## A Brief Admonition to Go to Confession

We have always urged that confession should be voluntary and that the pope's tyranny should cease. As a result we are now rid of his coercion and set free from the intolerable load and burden that he laid upon Christendom. As we all know from experience, there had been no rule so burdensome as the one that forced everyone to go to confession on pain of committing the most serious of mortal sins. That law also placed on consciences the heavy burden and torture of having to enumerate all kinds of sin, so that no one was ever able to confess perfectly enough. The worst was that no one taught or even knew what confession might be or what help and comfort it could give. Instead, it was turned into sheer terror and a hellish torture that one had to go through even if one detested confession more than anything. These three oppressive things have now been lifted, and we have been granted the right to go to confession freely, under no pressure of coercion or fear; also, we are released from the torture of needing to enumerate all sins in detail; besides this we have the advantage of knowing how to make a beneficial use of confession for the comfort and strengthening of our consciences.

Everyone is now aware of this. But unfortunately people have learned it only too well. They do as they please and apply their freedom wrongfully as if it meant that they ought not or must not go to confession. For we readily understand whatever is to our advantage, and we find it especially easy to take in whatever is mild and gentle in the Gospel. But, as I have said, such pigs should not be allowed near the Gospel nor have any part of it. They should stay under the pope and let themselves continue to be driven and pestered to confess, to fast, and so on. For whoever does not want to believe the Gospel, live according to it, and do what a Christian ought to be doing, should not enjoy any of its benefits either. Imagine their wanting to enjoy only the benefits, without accepting any of the responsibilities or investing anything of themselves—what sort of thing is that! We do not want to make preaching available for that sort nor to grant permission that our liberty and its enjoyment be opened up to them; instead, we will let the pope and the likes of him take over and force them to his will, genuine tyrant that he is. The rabble that will not obey the Gospel deserves nothing else than that kind of a jailer who is God's devil and hangman. But to others who gladly hear the Gospel we must keep on preaching, admonishing, encouraging, and coaxing them not to forget the precious and comforting treasure offered in the Gospel. Therefore we here intend to say also a few words about confession in order to instruct and admonish the uninformed.

In the first place, I have said that besides the confession here being considered there are two other kinds, which may even more properly be called the Christians' common confession. They are [1] the confession and plea for forgiveness made to God alone and [2] the confession that is made to the neighbor alone. These two kinds of confession are included in the Lord's Prayer, in which we pray, "Forgive us our trespasses, as we forgive those who trespass against us," etc. In fact, the entire Lord's Prayer is nothing else than such a confession. For what are our petitions other than a confession that we neither have nor do what we ought, as well as a plea for grace and a cheerful conscience? Confession of this sort should and must continue without letup as long as we live. For the Christian way essentially consists in acknowledging ourselves to be sinners and in praying for grace.

Similarly, the other of the two confessions, the one that every Christian makes to his neighbor, is also included in the Lord's Prayer. For here we mutually confess our guilt and our desire for forgiveness to each other before coming before God and begging for His forgiveness. Now, all of us are guilty of sinning against one another; therefore we may and should publicly confess this before everyone without shrinking in one another's presence. For what the proverb says is true, "If anyone is perfect, then all are"; there is no one at all who fulfills his obligations toward God and his neighbor. Besides such universal guilt there is, however, also the particular guilt of the person who has provoked another to rightful anger and needs to ask his pardon. Thus we have in the Lord's Prayer a double absolution: there we are forgiven both our offenses against God and those against our neighbor, and there we forgive our neighbor and become reconciled to him.

Besides this public, daily, and necessary confession, there is also the confidential confession that is only made before a single brother. If something particular weighs upon us or troubles us, something with which we keep torturing ourselves and can find no rest, and we do not find our faith to be strong enough to cope with it, then this private form of confession gives us the opportunity of laying the matter before some brother and receiving counsel, comfort, and strength when and however often we wish. That we should do this is not included in any divine command, as are the other two kinds of confession. Rather, it is offered to everyone who may need it, as an opportunity to be used by him as his need requires. The origin and establishment of private confession lies in the fact that Christ Himself placed His absolution into the hands of His Christian people with the command that they should absolve one another of their sins. Thus any heart that feels its sinfulness and desires consolation has here a sure refuge when he hears God's Word and makes the discovery that God through a human being looses and absolves him from his sins.

So notice, then, that confession, as I have often said, consists of two parts. The first is my own work and action, when I lament my sin and desire comfort and refreshment for my soul. The other part is a work that God does when He declares me free of my sin through His Word placed in the mouth of a man. It is this splendid, noble thing that makes confession so lovely, so comforting. It used to be that we emphasized it only as a work of ours; all that we were then concerned about was whether our act of confession was pure and perfect in every detail. We paid no attention to the second and most necessary part of confession, nor did we proclaim it; we acted just as if confession were nothing but a good work by which payment was to be made to God, so that if the confession was inadequate and not exactly correct in every detail, then the absolution would not be valid and the sin unforgiven. Thereby the people were driven to the point where everyone had to despair of making so pure a confession (an obvious impossibility) and where no one could feel at ease in his conscience or have confidence in his absolution. Thus they not only rendered the precious confession useless to us but also made it a bitter burden causing noticeable spiritual harm and ruin.

In our view of confession, therefore, we should sharply separate its two parts far from each other. We should place slight value on our part in it. But God's Word in the absolution part of confession we should hold in high and great esteem. We should not proceed as if we intended to perform and offer to Him a splendid work, but simply to accept and receive something from Him. You dare not come saying how good or how bad you are. If you are a Christian, I in any case know well enough that you are; if you are not, I know that even better. But what you must see to is that you lament your problem and that you let yourself be helped to acquire a cheerful heart and conscience.

Moreover, no one may now pressure you with commandments. Rather, what we say is this: Whoever is a Christian or would like to be one is here faithfully advised to go and get the precious treasure. If you are no Christian and do not desire such comfort, we shall leave it to another to use force on you. By eliminating all need for the pope's tyranny, command, and coercion, we cancel them with a single sweep. As I have said, we teach that whoever does not go to confession willingly and for the sake of obtaining the absolution, he may as well forget about it. Yes, and whoever goes around relying on the purity of his act of making confession, let him stay away. Nevertheless, we strongly urge you by all means to make confession of your need, not with the intention of thereby doing a worthy work but in order to hear what God has arranged for you to be told. What I am saying is that you are to concentrate on the Word, on the absolution, to regard it as a great and precious and magnificently splendid treasure, and to accept it with all praise and thanksgiving to God.

If this were explained in detail and if the need that ought to move and induce us to make confession were pointed out, then one would need little urging or coercion, for everyone's own conscience would so drive and disturb him that he would be glad to do what a poor and miserable beggar does when he hears that a rich gift of money or clothing is being handed out at a certain place; so as not to miss it, he would run there as fast as he can and would need no bailiff to beat and drive him on. Now, suppose that in place of the invitation one were to substitute a command to the effect that all beggars should run to that place but would not say why nor mention what they should look for and receive there. What else would the beggar do but make the trip with distaste, without thinking of going to get a gift but simply of letting people see what a poor, miserable beggar he is? This would bring him little joy and comfort but only greater resentment against the command that was issued.

Exactly so the pope's preachers kept silent in the past about the splendid gift and inexpressible treasure to be had through confession. All they did was to drive people in crowds to confession, with no further aim than to let them see what impure, dirty people they were. Who could go willingly to confession under such circumstances? We, however, do not say that people should look at you to see how filthy you are, using you as a mirror to preen themselves. Rather, we give this counsel: If you are poor and miserable, then go to confession and make use of its healing medicine. He who feels his misery and need will no doubt develop such a longing for it that he will run toward it with joy. But those who pay no attention to it and do not come of their own accord, we let them go their way. Let them be sure of this, however, that we do not regard them as Christians.

Thus we teach what a splendid, precious, and comforting thing confession is. Moreover, we strongly urge people not to despise a blessing which in view of our great need is so priceless. Now, if you are a Christian, then you do not need either my pressuring or the pope's orders, but you will undoubtedly compel yourself to come to confession and will beg me for a share in it. However, if you want to despise it and proudly continue without confession, then we must draw the conclusion that you are no Christian and should not enjoy the Sacrament either. For you despise what no Christian should despise and you thereby bring it about that you cannot have forgiveness of your sins. This is a sure sign that you also despise the Gospel.

To sum it up, we want to have nothing to do with coercion. However, if someone does not listen to or follow our preaching and its warning, we will have nothing to do with him, nor may he have any share in the Gospel. If you were a Christian, then you ought to be happy to run more than a hundred miles to confession and not let yourself be urged to come; you should rather come and compel us to give you the opportunity. For in this matter the compulsion must be the other way around: we must act under orders, you must come into freedom. We pressure no one, but we let ourselves be pressured, just as we let people compel us to preach and to administer the Sacrament.

When I therefore urge you to go to confession, I am doing nothing else than urging you to be a Christian. If I have brought you to the point of being a Christian, I have thereby also brought you to confession. For those who really desire to be true Christians, to be rid of their sins, and to have a cheerful conscience already possess the true hunger and thirst. They reach for the bread, just as Psalm 42:1 says of a

126

hunted hart, burning in the heat with thirst, "As a hart longs for flowing streams, so longs my soul for Thee, O God." In other words, as a hart with anxious and trembling eagerness strains toward a fresh, flowing stream, so I yearn anxiously and tremblingly for God's Word, absolution, the Sacrament, etc. See, that would be teaching aright concerning confession, and people could be given such a desire and love for it that they would come and run after us for it, more than we would like. Let the papists plague and torment themselves and others who pass up the treasure and exclude themselves from it. Let us, however, lift our hands in praise and thanksgiving to God for having graciously brought us to this our understanding of confession.

# Study
# Questions

MARTIN LUTHER'S PREFACE

1. What classes of people aroused Luther's high and healthy anger because of their attitude toward the teaching of Christian doctrine?
2. What was Luther's personal habitual use of the Catechism? What benefits would any Christian today experience from a similar habit?
3. What directive does Luther find for us in Deuteronomy 6:7-8?
4. What promise can be made to those who diligently use the Catechism?
5. What is Luther's admonition to family heads in his shorter preface?
6. For which adults first of all did Luther intend his Catechism? For the benefit of which two kinds of beginners in Christianity should these adults learn and use the Catechism?

THE TEN COMMANDMENTS

*The First Commandment*

1. Does the wording of the First Commandment support the statement that "decent god*less* people" nevertheless do have gods whom they serve?
2. What is it to *have* a god? What does God mean when He says we are to have Him alone as our God? What is our attitude toward Him to be?
3. Give a close description of some popular false gods of our generation and how an idolatrous heart feels and behaves toward each.

4. Describe the change in the heart that would have to take place for someone to turn from his false gods to serving the one and only God.
5. Is it true that "the world practices nothing but false worship and idolatry"? Support your answer. How do you reconcile the above quotation with the fact that worship of graven images is quite rare today?
6. Make a list of all religions that do not worship the Triune God and yet forbid the worship of graven images. Are these religions allowed or forbidden by the First Commandment? Why?
7. What is "work-righteousness," also called "self-righteousness"? Explain why the Catechism calls it "the height of idolatry."
8. "We are to trust in God alone, look to Him, and expect to receive nothing but good things from Him." What connection does this statement have with the First Commandment?
9. The Catechism lists a great many kinds of good things that come to us from God. Add to the list other and modern things that are real blessings. Trace any of the blessings you enjoy back through their various sources and keep asking who is to have the credit and get the appreciation. If in your heart you give the credit and your real appreciation to someone or something else than the true God, what are you guilty of?
10. Notice the questions Luther offers for testing whether we have the one true God as our God. As you honestly test yourself, how do you come out? Only Jesus, the Son of God, who became your Brother to save you from sin and its penalties, passed the test perfectly. What does the perfect righteousness of Jesus do for you?
11. Why is Exodus 20:5b-6 attached to the First Commandment although it applies to all the commandments?
12. What examples from our own time show that the anger and punishment of God is directed against those who despise Him? When did the "God is dead" idea begin? What evils have been spreading since then? Apply Roman 1:18 ff. to this situation. Find other similar divine threats in the Bible.
13. What divine promise in Exodus 20:5-6 is stronger than the threats of divine wrath? Compare Romans 3:21-26; 5:8-10, 18-21; 6:23. Find other such Gospel promises in the Bible.
14. What are the threats and promises of God meant to accomplish in our lives?
15. How do our observations sometimes seem to contradict what God says in His threats and promises? What is the explanation for the seeming contradiction between what God has said and what we observe?
16. What is Luther's point when he compares a person who uses God's earthly gifts with love and reverence toward God to a shoemaker or a hotel guest? Invent other comparisons to make the same point.


*The Second Commandment*

1. The aim of the First Commandment is to point out the right relationship of the heart to God. What is the aim of the Second Commandment?
2. Explain what is meant by misuse of God's name. Give present day examples of the way people sinfully connect references to God or to the things of God (for example, His Scripture words) with something false and sinful.
3. Are the Catechism examples of misuse of God's name still pertinent? Explain.
4. Luther says that the greatest misuse of God's name occurs in spiritual matters involving the conscience. What does he mean?
5. What is "pluming oneself with God's name"? How is God's name often misused in matters of faith and doctrine? What is blasphemy? Give

modern instances of such misuses of God's name and Word.

6. In summarizing the ways God's name is misused, what specific sins does Luther name?

7. What is the positive side of the Second Commandment, that is, what does it command us to do? Give Bible examples of persons joyfully doing these things.

8. Is swearing oaths by God's name forbidden, commanded, or both? Explain. Give examples from the Bible and from modern life of both sinful and God-pleasing oaths.

9. What connection is there between the teaching of the true doctrines of God's Word, namely the Scriptures, and the Second Commandment? between prayer and the Second Commandment?

10. What twofold approach does Luther urge when training children to observe this commandment? What specific habits does he find desirable? What benefits will come from them?

11. Discuss ways of applying Luther's principles for training children in reverent use of God's name.

## The Third Commandment

1. What was the "external observance" of the Sabbath that the Third Commandment required of all Old Testament believers? Name some other "Old Testament regulations that are bound to specific customs, times, and places" (i.e., other O. T. ceremonial laws).

2. Give two reasons for observing "holy days" in the New Testament. What should be a Christian's response to the idea that certain days are more holy or sacred in themselves than others? Where in the New Testament did Christ and His Holy Spirit abolish the "external" regulations that were once connected with the Third Commandment?

3. To sanctify means to keep holy. How are holy days to be kept holy? Compare various common styles of Sunday observance and rate them as to their holiness or unholiness.

4. What is able to make a person's whole life and labor God-pleasing and holy? How does the correct answer to this question relate to the observance of the Third Commandment in the New Testament sense?

5. If the holiness or goodness of a work depends on whether the person doing the work is holy (that is, in a right relationship to God), it is clearly most vital that he be holy and in that right relationship. How can this be accomplished? Only by God Himself? Through what means? Through His Word? His Word of the Law? His Word of the Gospel? What benefit does God intend for us by commanding us to sanctify or keep holy the holy day?

6. In what ways does Luther see people violating the Commandment on any given day of worship? What are some of the modern counterparts of these desecrations of the Lord's Day?

7. What is the deadly sin of acedia? How prevalent is it today? Is it present in our own lives?

8. What does Luther mean by saying that we spend our lives in the devil's territory? What will guarantee a person's sure defeat by his old evil foe? Where can he find the power to show the devil the door and turn him out of his life? What, then, must he do in keeping with the Third Commandment?

## The Fourth Commandment

1. What value does God place on the parental state as compared with other stations in life? How do you know? Why does "honoring" involve more than "loving"? In what ways are parents God's earthly representatives?

2. How can one honor one's parents by one's attitude? by one's speech? by one's conduct?
3. In God's eyes how does honoring one's parents compare with "spiritual" works?
4. What satisfaction will young people have if they concentrate above all on obedience to this commandment?
5. Give modern instances of the blessings that a child's obedience brings to his parents; to the child himself; to society.
6. How does the Fourth Commandment rate in importance when compared with the first three? Why? How does it rank when compared with the rest of the commandments? Why?
7. How should gratitude for benefits received from one's parents be made publicly visible? Does this always happen? What is needed to make it happen?
8. What is God's promise to those who keep the Fourth Commandment? What happens when this commandment is scorned? What happens to families that through the generations respect this commandment?
9. What connection is there between parental authority and other kinds of authority?
10. Discuss the significance of this commandment for servants and masters, for employers and employees, for citizens and governmental authorities.
11. What evidence do you see in modern life "that everyone wants to be his own master, accountable to no superior, caring about no one, and doing only what pleases himself"? What is "the way God punishes one scoundrel by means of another"?
12. When "we grumble about disloyalties, power plays, and injustice," Luther wants us to remember that "we ourselves are rascals who thoroughly deserve such punishment and yet are not in the least improved by it." Is this charge true? Discuss.
13. What three classes of fathers has the *Large Catechism* named so far? Which class of fathers remains? How were "spiritual fathers" who applied God's Word treated in Luther's day? How are they often treated today? Does the point that the *Large Catechism* makes about meager support for the livelihood of pastors apply today? What should be a Christian's attitude toward shepherds of souls? Why?
14. Does the Fourth Commandment imply any duties and responsibilities on the part of parents and other superiors? What sinful attitudes do parents often have toward children? masters and employers toward servants or employees? the governing toward those governed? What are the blessings from God for parents and superiors who carry out their responsibilities?


*The Fifth Commandment*

1. Why is this commandment placed after and not before the Fourth Commandment? What does the Table of Duties of the *Small Catechism* say under the heading "Of Civil Government"? Discuss the point that what is forbidden here does not apply to rulers when carrying out their proper functions.
2. In what obvious ways, other than actual violence and bloodshed, is this commandment most often transgressed? Are anger and hatred as serious in God's sight as murder? See Matthew 5:20-26. Why is it that the rightful anger of parents and other human authorities is not forbidden in the Fifth Commandment, but is actually a duty?
3. How necessary is this commandment for human well-being? List various kinds of temptation to disregard this commandment. What is the source of the human desire to repay evil with evil, i.e., to take revenge? Of what help is this commandment to overcome that desire?

4. What three kinds of "killing" does Luther explain as being transgressions of this commandment? Does the world regard all three of them in the same way that Christians do? Explain the fact that non-Christians know certain things to be wrong (see Romans 2:14-15). Why do they not recognize as wrong everything that God has forbidden?
5. How does Luther explain and then prove from Scripture that to neglect opportunities to help someone who is in bodily need amounts to the same thing as killing him?
6. Prove that kindness to one's enemies is commanded in this commandment. Give Bible examples of love shown to enemies. Who showed us undeserved love and kindness despite our hostility toward Him? (See Romans 5:10; also recall God's attitude toward us as explained earlier under the First Commandment.) When we believe this and rejoice in it, what effect does this have on our attitude toward those who do us harm or wish us ill?
7. Why does the *Large Catechism* stress the importance of realizing "that the true, holy, divine works are those that God's Word commands. . . . The reverse is true of all saintliness devised by men"? In a world so full of obvious hatreds and violence, is it still necessary to teach that saintliness devised by men is "but stench and filth, deserving of nothing but wrath and damnation"? Does the story of the Pharisee and the publican contribute anything to the answer to this question? If so, how?

*The Sixth Commandment*

1. Since the first three commandments all concern love toward God and since the last six commandments all proceed from one "central point" in Luther's view, does this not leave the Fourth Commandment in a bridging position? Discuss the significance of this position of God's representatives on earth for the training of a family and of a people in reverence toward God on the one hand and in regard for the fellow man on the other.
2. How does Luther explain the emphasis of the Sixth Commandment on adultery as representing all the forms of unchastity? How comprehensive does He find this commandment to be in its prohibitions? In its demands?
3. How does this commandment involve concern for the welfare of the neighbor?
4. How would you explain the statement that God sanctioned marriage already in the Fourth Commandment? How does the Sixth Commandment add to this sanctioning?
5. Contrast the two following statements: (1) marriage was an evolutionary development; (2) marriage was instituted by God, as recorded in Genesis.
6. Compare current negative attitudes toward marriage with God's regard for it as "something splendid" and as a means of highest service to the world through the promotion of the "knowledge of God, godly life, and virtue of every kind." In what way had medieval teaching undermined the high estimate that God's Word places on the estate of matrimony?
7. If, contrary to this commandment, medieval religion promoted vows of chastity outside of marriage, what kind of life-styles detrimental to marriage are promoted by modern nonreligion? How does the Sixth Commandment apply in either instance?
8. What means are available to "again turn the situation around to the point where marriage would again be honored"?
9. Within marriage, what is the key for maintaining a chaste and healthy appreciation and use of sexuality in one's thinking, speech, and behavior? If mutual love and respect are the basis for a happy marriage, what is the basis and source of such marital love and respect?

### The Seventh Commandment

1. With the aim of protecting people's property, what has God forbidden in this commandment? How is stealing here defined? Make a list of various ways of acquiring the property of others by unjust means such as are used by criminals; by shopkeepers; by servicemen; by clerks; by business men; by employees; by mechanics; by workmen; by the "decent citizens" who operate as "swivel chair swindlers." Comment on the statement that "thievery . . . is the most common craft and the largest trade union on earth."
2. What are the difficulties in apprehending thieves, embezzlers, racketeers? in bringing charges against shady dealers? in confronting neighbors and acquaintances when they deal unfairly with us?
3. What justification was there for the charge that the holy see at Rome "by thievery has taken over the treasures of the world"? Name some obvious modern "charitable" and "religious" movements that are milking multitudes of their money by misrepresentation, deception, religious fraud, and false teachings.
4. How does the language of the *Large Catechism* reflect the wrath of God against thieving rascals and cheating scoundrels?
5. Since most dishonesty, pilfering, and neglect of an employer's interests on the part of employees goes undetected, how can the *Large Catechism* say to the guilty that they "will get paid in kind" for what they have done? If workmen and laborers are left to "rip off people" by overcharging them, how can it be said that God will repay them "according to their deserts"? What of a person in business who raises prices "as if he had the right . . . to sell at whatever exorbitant price he wishes"? Can God be trusted to "take matters into His own hands" as the Catechism says He will? Does the "enjoyment" of ill-gotten gains give joy in the true and lasting sense? Comment on known modern instances of personal misery and a deplorable end for godless gougers.
6. What is to be a Christian's attitude toward those who have cheated and robbed him? Why may impenitent thieves and cheats take no comfort from such a Christian spirit of forgiveness? What is the outlook for anyone who takes advantage of the poor and the meek?
7. How far does the responsibility of the church go in opposing dishonesty and thievery? What is the responsibility of government and law-enforcement agencies?
8. The *Large Catechism* strongly emphasizes the negative aspects of this commandment. Why this emphasis? Is the positive side less important? What is the positive side? Give a number of Biblical examples of people giving aid to others in matters of property. What are the blessings and promises attached to obeying this commandment? Cite Biblical and modern instances of divine blessing on those seeking the neighbor's material welfare.

### The Eighth Commandment

1. How does a person's reputation affect his standing in society?
2. Of what importance is testimony in court for protecting or destroying a person's good name? Why, in Luther's view, is false or misleading testimony in court likely to occur under orderly governments where justice prevails?
3. What kind of person should a judge be? Why?
4. What must the primary concern of a judge or a witness be? Against what kind of temptations must a lawyer be on guard?
5. How does the world transgress this commandment in its opinion of Christians and godly preachers? In what ways is the Word of God itself made the object of false witness? Can you cite actual cases?

6. What are the implications of this commandment for our everyday conversations? Name and examine in the light of God's Word various kinds of false and pernicious uses of the tongue. How are we to judge the pleasure we take in having our ears tickled by scandalmongering or slanderous gossip?

7. When is it a grave sin and when, on the other hand, is it a solemn duty publicly to judge and reprove another person's sins? Whose authority does a scandalmonger invade?

8. What is to be said in response to the argument, "Why can't I talk about it if it is true"? Why is it that "no one should make public or assert as being true anything that is not already public and supported by sufficient evidence"? May public offenses be referred to publicly?

9. Why may, indeed must, civil authorities, preacher, and parents judge and condemn current sins?

10. What guidance does Jesus give in Matthew 18:15-17? How can we apply this passage to someone who comes whispering another's secret faults to us?

11. "Do you imagine that it is something insignificant to gain a brother?" Discuss this question. If helping a person change his wrong ways is a good and important thing, what would be the least effective approach? What would be the most effective approach?

12. What is the great difference between the way to deal with someone's secret sins and the way to deal with his public sins? Why, when false doctrine is taught, must it be publicly censured? By whom is this to be done?

13. How does Luther summarize the matter? What Scripture passage does he offer as motivation for keeping this commandment? Find other such passages

## The Ninth and Tenth Commandments

1. What particular applications did these commandments have in Old Testament Jewish life?

2. What kind of things are done under the guise of fair dealing by people who want what belongs to someone else yet do not want to appear dishonest? How does society aid and abet such practices?

3. What is the reason for the statement that this commandment is addressed to the most respectable people?

4. Name some specific maneuvers and shrewd practices approved by the world that come under the divine judgment of these commandments?

5. Is it still as true as Luther thought it was in his day that underhanded enticement of another's spouse is rare? Are clever tricks sometimes used today for purposes of seduction or of alienation of affection?

6. Can you identify any deceptive claims and other tricks used today in order to lure clients, customers, and workers away from their previous loyalties?

7. What is often our attitude and feeling when the neighbor succeeds, prospers, or finds happiness? What does our Father in heaven want our attitude to be?

8. Is it a moral requirement, that is to say, is it God's will that we take positive action to help our neighbor in matters of money and property? Or is it optional? Give Biblical and modern instances of such help freely and gladly given.

## Conclusion of the Ten Commandments

1. What are the other chief parts of Christian doctrine, without which it is impossible to do what the first chief part teaches? Why are they necessary?

2. What divine threat against transgressors is attached to the Ten Commandments? What divine promise is attached?
3. How do we know that God requires more than external conformity to the Commandments? What does He require?
4. Why is the First Commandment called the "fountainhead and source" of all others?
5. Why were the Ten Commandments to be everywhere displayed in Old Testament times? Could anything similar be done today for the same purpose?

THE CREED

1. Why is it essential to learn the teachings of the Creed if one wants to know God? Why is the same thing necessary if one wants to take the Ten Commandments seriously?
2. Why do you suppose the medieval church divided the Apostles' Creed into 12 parts? Why is Luther's division into 3 parts a great improvement?

*The First Article*

1. If anyone were to ask you to describe God, what might you answer to begin with?
2. What is the connection between the First Article of the Creed and the First Commandment?
3. List as many kinds of things as possible that have their source in God's creaive power and love.
4. What words in the Creed imply the whole caring, protecting, preserving activity of God? List aspects of this activity. Discuss God's motive for all this and the kind of God this shows Him to be.
5. What evidence is there to show that we humans rarely put our trust in the truth confessed in he First Article?
6. Why would it humble and terrify us if we really and fully believed the First Article? What kinds of sins would we begin to notice in ourselves?
7. How should we use our daily experiences to impress on ourselves the truth confessed in the First Article? Why does God keep doing for us all the countless things that belong to our welfare? What does He thereby wish to show us about His feelings toward us? What is meant by the statement that "the Father has given Himself to us together with everything of His making"? What was His greatest Gift, the Gift to be considered under the Second Article?

*The Second Article*

1. What is meant by the statement that the Son of God "poured Himself out completely for us not withholding anything of Himself from us"?
2. What do you include when in faith you confess that "Jesus Christ became my Lord"? Describe the various foes from whose terrible lordship Christ redeemed you in order to become your gracious Lord.
3. How did we get into the situation of needing to be redeemed? What would God's attitude toward us be forever if His Son had not redeemed us?
4. The lords we had before Christ Jesus became our Savior and Lord are called "tyrant jailors." Why?
5. What did Christ do to make Himself our Lord of righteousness, life, and every blessing? As a result of what Christ did, how does God now feel toward us—what is His attitude toward us?
6. What basis is there for saying that "the little word 'Lord' simply means as much as Redeemer"? What four aspects of meaning does the *Large Catechism* find in the word "Redeemer"? Explain each of the four.

7. The other parts of the Second Article are said to "explain and underscore the manner and the means by which the redemption came about." Take each of those parts separately and on the basis of Scripture consider what role each part plays in Christ's work of redemption.
8. What is very much needed in addition to the discussion in the *Large Catechism* if the people in a Christian congregation are to have a detailed explanation of all the individual points covered in the Second Article of the Apostles' Creed? (For a survey of these points examine the questions and answers under the Second Article in the synodical Catechism.)

*The Third Article*

1. What is meant by the "work of sanctification"? Through what means does the Holy Spirit accomplish it?
2. In and through what company of people is the Holy Spirit working in order to bring individuals to Christ? What is the one and only means through which He does this?
3. What is the good news that the Gospel proclaims? Do the benefits of Christ's redeeming work reach anyone without the Gospel? What is the Gospel's importance for the salvation of the individual? for bringing him to faith in Christ and to a knowledge of what He did as mankind's Redeemer?
4. What is the Holy Spirit's work in connection with Gospel proclamation? What does He offer and give in and through the Gospel? How is the work of sanctification, of making holy, connected with this?
5. Explain how the Christian church is the mother of every Christian.
6. What happens to the Spirit's work (of making people holy by putting them in a right relationship with God through faith in Christ) whenever the preaching of the Gospel is "shoved under the bench"? But suppose that all kinds of "holy works" are promoted despite the absence of the Holy Spirit and His Gospel—who is it that is active in promoting them?
7. What various meanings of the term "church" must be distinguished from each other?
8. Note carefully the Large Catechism's description of the church in the sense in which the Apostles' Creed uses the term. Is there any visible church body, any denominational grouping, or even any Christendom that corresponds to that description? Is the perception of the reality and existence of the one church at all a matter of sight, of headcounting? Is it a matter of faith, then, of "the evidence of things not seen"? On what is our faith in the existence of a definite number of true believers in Christ based?
9. What would be the marks or the evidences of the presence and activity of the church?
10. What is the supreme treasure given by the Holy Spirit to everyone who by faith in Christ as his saving Lord is within the one church? How can this treasure be kept and enjoyed? What would happen to our faith's grip on this treasure if we ceased to hear and receive the Gospel through Word and Sacrament?
11. Christ died for all the world. Why, then, does nobody outside of the church possess God's forgiveness?
12. Why does "the resurrection of the body and the life everlasting" also come under the Holy Spirit's work of making Christ's people holy?
13. How does the Creed help us to "understand the nature, mind, and activity of God"?
14. In what way is the Apostles' Creed a dividing line between the two parts of the human race?

15. What exactly is the great difference between the teachings of the Ten Commandments and the teachings of the Creed?

## THE LORD'S PRAYER

1. How does the Lord's Prayer relate in general to the Creed and to the Ten Commandments? What is the specific connection between the Second Commandment and the Lord's Prayer?
2. How does genuine prayer differ from a "babbling and droning" and "external repetition"?
3. When Christians find perverse thoughts about prayer arising in the heart, how are they to counteract such thinking? Do God's commandments, then, give guidance and direction also to Christians? Which use of the Law is this?
4. How does God regard genuine prayer? How should our view of Christian prayer differ from the world's opinion of it?
5. What are some false motives for praying? What are some good reasons for praying? Can you remember some specific instances when you were consciously aware of these reasons encouraging and impelling you to pray?
6. When is prayer genuine?
7. What kinds of things should we ask for for ourselves? for others? Who are some of the others who need our prayers?
8. What are some of the hindrances to prayer? Who is the most bitter foe of prayer and why? What weapon against this foe did Jesus teach us to use?

### The First Petition

1. Since God's name is always holy in itself, what is the purpose of this petition? Why does God's name concern every child of God from the moment he is reborn in Holy Baptism? Why is God's name our greatest treasure?
2. In this petition we are praying that we and others may never bring disgrace but only honor to our God, who shared His name with us when He took us into His family. What are two ways in which it becomes evident whether we are bringing disgrace or honor to the name we bear as children of God?
3. When does "Christian" preaching and teaching bring the worst possible disgrace and dishonor to the name of God? When do hearers and learners become guilty of perpetuating that dishonor?
4. To what other sins of the tongue do people often attach God's name, thereby dishonoring His name? Why do they thus become guilty in each instance of a double sin?
5. How are the Ten Commandments a means of testing whether a given act or mode of behavior by a professed follower of God disgraces the holy name he bears?
6. Discuss the positive ways in which our speech and conduct will increasingly bring honor to God's name if we genuinely pray the First Petition and receive God's answer to it through the Holy Spirit's sanctifying influence.
7. What is the very close connection between the First Petition and the Second Commandment?
8. What motivation for sincerely praying that God's name be kept holy do you find in your own needs and in the needs of those around you?

### The Second Petition

1. What is the nature of the kingdom or rulership of God that has been established by Christ and is being spread by His Holy Spirit?

2. What is the means the Holy Spirit uses to extend God's reign over a human heart and life? When does that reign begin?
3. What is the value of the blessing for which we pray in the Second Petition? How can a believer's enjoyment of the blessing be increased during his life on earth? Describe the change that eternity will bring to his enjoyment of this blessing.
4. Conduct a minisurvey among your Christian friends asking whether they ever pray for "everything that belongs to God Himself." Then ask whether they have every prayed the Second Petition. Could this lead into a discussion of the content of the petition?
5. What is the point of the illustration in which an emperor orders a beggar to ask for anything he may wish, at which the beggar requests nothing but a ladle of soup?
6. How will a person's faith or unfaith in God's promise (namely to give His greatest gifts when asked) affect his response to the Lord's invitation to pray the Second Petition?

## The Third Petition

1. When the treasures we pray for in the First and Second Petitions come into our lives, what robbery attempts may we expect?
2. Why is the devil so furiously intent on obstructing the fulfillment of the first two petitions?
3. Can you think of some specific examples showing how both our sinful nature (flesh, old Adam) and the Christless world serve as the devil's allies in trying to hinder the hallowing of God's name and the coming of His kingdom's blessings?
4. Describe the Christian self-denial and crossbearing that must follow when we receive the treasures we ask for in the first two petitions.
5. In the face of the three-pronged attack from devil, world, and flesh, what weapon of defense does the Lord offer to you and teach you to pray for in the Third Petition? Why must the fulfillment of God's will necessarily defend our possession of the priceless blessings we receive from God's name and God's kingdom?
6. What is the connection between our praying in the Third Petition for defense against our spiritual foes and God's command to us in the Third Commandment that we should let Him train us in the knowledge and use of His Word?

## The Fourth Petition

1. What "wide area" does this petition cover?
2. How does modern experience bear out the statement that when praying for the preservation of life and its well-being the greatest need probably is to pray "for our civil authorities and government"?
3. If good government is so important in providing for "that poor breadbox, the needs of our body and of our earthly life," find a connection between the Fourth Petition and the Fourth Commandment.
4. The *Large Catechism* names only a few of the kinds of things that God provides for our physical life and well-being. From our 20th century's wider awareness of the necessities of life, add to the list. What is the ultimate source of life and its maintenance? How aware is modern man of this?
5. What kinds of aims and activities of the devil caused Luther to realize that he is the worst foe, most intent on destroying our earthly blessings, and that the Fourth Petition is a protective wall against him?
6. What does the fact that God instructs us to pray this petition show about His concern and care for our earthly existence?

*The Fifth Petition*

1. What connection does this petition have with all of the Ten Commandments? What connection does it have with the Gospel in Word and Sacraments?
2. If by means of the Gospel the Holy Spirit "daily and richly forgives all sins to me and all believers," why is there need for praying this petition?
3. How does this petition serve God's purpose to break our pride and foster humility?
4. What does this petition do for giving us "a happy and cheerful conscience able to stand before God in prayer"?
5. With what understanding does God grant and must we receive the answer to this prayer for forgiveness?
6. Does this petition in any way imply that we are forgiven by God on account of the forgiveness we grant our neighbor? Carefully explain your answer. Why is it that our forgiveness of our neighbor and God's forgiveness granted to us are linked together in this petition?

*The Sixth Petition*

1. What bearing does this petition have on our obedience to the Ten Commandments?
2. What is "the flesh"? Why is it a constant source of temptation in a Christian's life? Name and discuss some of the temptations associated with each of the commandments that clearly have their source in the flesh.
3. Name and discuss temptations connected with each of the commandments that clearly have their source in the unbelieving, God-scorning world.
4. Name and discuss temptations involving the conscience and spiritual matters by which the devil aims to turn us against God and His Word. What Biblical examples are there of persons who fell into the sins named in this connection in the Catechism?
5. Do all the above temptations permanently cease when God answers this petition? In what manner, then, does God grant this prayer?
6. Did Jesus in giving us this petition mean us to ask that we might never feel temptations? Did He, the God-man, ever feel the shafts of actual temptations? If He did, what might we expect to feel any day, any time?
7. What help and refuge have we when tempted so that we do not become trapped and destroyed through surrendering to the temptation? Can you give Biblical or personal examples of temptations overcome in God's strength with God's Word and with the weapon of prayer?

*The Seventh Petition*

1. What is the Greek form of this petition? Does the English form exclude or include a plea for deliverance from the Evil One?
2. What are the major kinds of evil? Who and what is ultimately the cause and source of all such evils in the world? Is that source and that cause still active today? In what sense are disasters of all kinds caused by the devil? (See the Book of Job.)
3. In the midst of life's ills and troubles, what assurance of God's love and concern is there in His teaching us to pray the Seventh Petition?
4. What significance does Luther see in the placement of this commandment at the end of the Lord's Prayer?
5. What is the meaning of "Amen"? What is the significance of ending a prayer with "Amen"?
6. Why is the attitude expressed in the "Amen" absolutely necessary for true prayer and for God's granting our petitions? What would the

opposite attitude do to our praying? Support your answers with words of Scripture.

## BAPTISM

1. Who established Christian baptism? What words of Christ are the basis of Christian baptism?
2. Why is Baptism of priceless worth and not something optional despite its "external form"?
3. Who really baptized you? A pastor? God Himself? What proof have you?
4. Why does the *Large Catechism* emphasize that even the most splendidly glittering works devised by human beings would not be as noble as God's action in picking up a straw?
5. Explain the *Large Catechism's* answer to the question, What is Baptism?
6. How might one answer someone who says, "How can a handful of water help a soul?"
7. What priceless treasure has God combined with the water of Baptism? How are we therefore to think of the water when this treasure is joined to it in Baptism?
8. How does Augustine define a sacrament?
9. Why dare not these two, Word and water, be separated from each other, neither in the baptismal action nor in our understanding of it?
10. What is "the power, effect, benefit, fruit, and purpose of Baptism"? How do you know this is the effect? What produces this effect? In what words does Titus 3:5 indicate this effect?
11. How can one answer those who say that since faith alone saves, therefore the baptismal action does nothing toward a person's salvation? What is our answer when Baptism is discounted on the ground that it is something external?
12. Who are the baptized persons who actually receive the benefits of Baptism? Which baptized persons throw away its benefits? How do you know?
13. What places the pearl of forgiveness and salvation into every single Baptism performed according to Christ's ordinance? What is necessary for receiving, taking, holding, and having that pearl?
14. Some might object that since salvation is a matter of faith and that it cannot be gained by human works, therefore Baptism, being a work or action, cannot save. How would you, remembering whose work or action a Baptism really is, answer them?
15. What are the three points concerning Baptism that the *Large Catechism* has dealt with so far?
16. Why is it a lifelong task to learn, hold to, and truly apply God's teaching about Baptism?
17. How is a person to regard and rightly use his Baptism day by day? What does such use do for body and soul? What is the explanation for such wonderful effects of Baptism in the believer's life?

### Infant Baptism

1. What conclusion about the validity of infant Baptism is to be drawn from the fact that many who were baptized as infants had the Holy Spirit? from the fact that the church has never ceased and will never cease to exist?
2. On what does the validity of a Baptism depend? On the faith of the recipient? Or on the Word and promise of God? Like an inheritance that is not claimed, what does a person's Baptism keep in store for him even if he refuses to use it and benefit from it?
3. How does the validity of Baptism compare with that of the Lord's Supper

in case a person receives it without faith? If the validity does not depend on the faith of the recipient, what happens to the argument that the Baptism of children is invalid because they do not believe?

4. Should a person be rebaptized if since his Baptism he despised the treasure of forgiveness, life, and salvation it had given him? Having finally learned the truth about Baptism and its benefit, what should he do?

5. On what basis are infants to be brought to be baptized?

6. In what way are those who deny the validity of infant Baptism blind to God's Word and command, blind to faith and obedience? What is the insurrectionist spirit Luther saw in those who regard Baptism as merely "water in the stream or in the bucket"?

7. What are the two daily events in a Christian's life that are symbolized in the baptismal action?

8. What is to happen every day with the Christian's old Adam and its pollutions? What is to arise daily in the Christian's life as from a watery grave?

9. Explain the statement, "If you live in repentance, you are progressing in your Baptism."

10. How long does a person's Baptism remain in force? Suppose a Christian falls into sin, loses faith in Christ, and forfeits his forgiveness. What is he then to do to be saved? Is he to be baptized over again? Or what?

11. What of the notion that the benefits of Baptism are forever lost if a person after Baptism has surrendered again to sin and unbelief? And what of the idea that "the second plank" in that case is repentance?

12. Explain what the *Large Catechism* teaches instead when it says to the person who has fallen out of the ship, out of his Baptism: "At once swim for the ship again."

13. Is your Baptism your "everyday wear"? Tell why you should and why you want to wear it constantly every day.


THE SACRAMENT OF THE ALTAR

1. Under what three headings may the Lord's Supper be considered? What is the basis for these three points?

2. What is the source of the Holy Supper's power and validity? Why do we insist that it is not the faith of the recipient that gives it its character?

3. On the basis of Scripture what is the Lutheran answer to the question, What is the Lord's Supper?

4. As in the case of Baptism, what is the importance of the principle, "When the Word is joined to the external element, it becomes a sacrament"?

5. What is the consequence of detaching the Word of Christ from the elements of bread and wine? What is present when the Word of Christ remains connected with the elements?

6. Is Christ's body and blood present in the Lord's Supper when some scoundrel receives or administers it? How do we know? Do unworthy, unbelieving, or wicked persons at the Lord's Table partake of Christ's true body and blood?

7. What is the power and benefit of the Lord's Supper? How do we know?

8. Why is the Lord's Supper fittingly called food for the soul? How does it strengthen and sustain in us a living faith in Christ as our Savior? What effect does this have on our living a new life of obedience toward Him? on our resistance against the devil's temptation?

9. How can one answer those who object that bread and wine cannot forgive sin and strengthen faith? Where was forgiveness acquired once and for all? What is the necessary means of communication to proclaim and convey this forgiveness and salvation to us? In addition to sending out word of that forgiveness for all to hear, Christ also connected that

forgiving word to the eating and drinking in the Lord's Supper. Show from His own words that this is so.

10. What does Christ say to every communicant about the body and blood he is eating and drinking? What assurance does this give to every communicant regarding God's forgiveness, grace, and love? What are the only two possible responses to that assurance?

11. When is a person completely ready to receive the blessings of the Lord's Supper? How are such preparations for Holy Communion as fasting and the like to be regarded?

12. What are some causes for the neglect of the Sacrament? What must be said of persons who absent themselves long from the Lord's Table?

13. What word of Christ concerning Holy Communion attendance will be followed gladly and willingly by everyone who wishes to be a Christian?

14. What is the inevitable final result of staying away repeatedly from the Lord's Supper? What is the alternative?

15. What mistake does the person make who stays away because he feels so unfit? What will happen if a person plans to wait until he feels no stings of conscience?

16. If disorderly and loose-living people want to come to the Lord's Table, what must they be told? Why? What, on the other hand, must those realize who are spiritually weak and acknowledge their frailties? Comment on the mistake of concentrating more on our own feeling than on Christ's command.

17. In addition to His command, what promise of Christ should powerfully urge us to receive the Lord's Supper often? Why is the Sacrament wholesome therapy not only for the soul but also for the mind and body?

18. Who are the only ones that receive the Sacrament to their harm? What is the good word for those who feel their personal problems hanging about their necks, are heavy laden with sins, fears, and temptation, and long for rescue?

19. What is the cure when my trouble is a numbness of spirit in which I feel no need and sense no hunger and thirst for the Sacrament? Figuratively speaking, would pinching myself help? What would that do? Or how about simply believing what God's Word says regarding my need? How about becoming aware of the ways of an evil world and the influence upon me of the Christless "decent godless people" with whom I am surrounded? How about a healthy awareness also of the reality of the devil and his wiles? Finally, if one still feels no need, who are the individuals whose aid and counsel I should seek? What is the value of counseling with some faithful Christian and asking him to help you analyze yourself? (Why will I most certainly be doomed to eternal destruction if I seek and follow the opinions and counsels of intellectually proud scorners of the teachings of Christ's Word and church?)

20. If adults realize the importance of the teachings of God's Word for themselves, what can they do to impress these things on the following generation?


*Confession*

1. What were the three aspects of medieval confession that made it a torturous burden?

2. To what other extreme did people's feelings regarding confession go when this tyranny was exposed? What is Luther's attitude toward those who want cheap grace, reaching only for "whatever is mild and gentle in the Gospel" while rejecting the strenuous truths about their responsibilities?

3. What are the three kinds of confession discussed in this section of the *Large Catechism*?

4. Describe the confession of sins to God that is built into the Lord's Prayer.
5. Describe the confession of sins to our neighbor that is built into the Lord's Prayer.
6. What is the difference between these two kinds of confession and a confession made privately before a single fellow Christian?
7. What are the two parts that belong to such a private confession? Which part is the "splendid, noble thing that makes confession so lovely, so comforting"?
8. What is the difference between our part in confession and God's part? On which of these parts should the overwhelming emphasis always be placed? What special term have we for God's wonderful part? Define absolution. What Scripture passages give God's people the authority to apply His forgiveness in Christ directly to individuals for removal of the guilt of specific sins?
9. Describe the sense of need that should urge a person to accept the invitation of God and receive the "precious and magnificently splendid treasure" in God's absolution as it is available in private confession.
10. Describe the *Large Catechism's* strong warnings against despising the treasure contained in confession and absolution, as well as the winsomeness of the invitation to receive God's amazing gift of grace.